ESSENTIAL

Prague: Regions and Best places to see

★ Best places to see 34–55

■ Featured sight

Staré Město Area 83–106

Josefov Area 134–146

Hradčany, Malá Strana and Beyond 107–133

Nové Město and Beyond 147–163

Original text by Christopher and Melanie Rice
Updated by Heather Maher

First published 2007.

ISBN-10: 0-7495-4967-X
ISBN-13: 978-0-7495-4967-1

Published by AA Publishing, a trading name of Automobile Association Developments Limited, whose registered office is Fanum House, Basing View, Basingstoke, Hampshire RG21 4EA.
Registered number 1878835.

A CIP catalogue record for this book is available from the British Library.

Colour separation: MRM Graphics Ltd
Printed and bound in Italy by Printer Trento S.r.l.

A02694
Maps in this title produced from mapping © MAIRDUMONT / Falk Verlag 2006

About this book

Symbols are used to denote the following categories:

- map reference to maps on cover
- address or location
- telephone number
- opening times
- restaurant or café on premises or nearby
- nearest underground train station
- nearest tram route
- nearest overground train station
- nearest ferry stop
- nearest airport
- admission charge
- other places of interest nearby
- other practical information
- ➤ indicates the page where you will find a fuller description

This book is divided into six sections.

The essence of Prague pages 6–19
Introduction; Features; Food and Drink; Short Break including the 10 Essentials

Planning pages 20–33
Before You Go; Getting There; Getting Around; Being There

Best places to see pages 34–55
The unmissable highlights of any visit to Prague

Best things to do pages 56–79
Places to have lunch; top activities; best views; speciality shops and more

Exploring pages 80–163
The best places to visit in Prague, organized by area

Excursions pages 164–183
Places to visit out of town

Maps
All map references are to the maps on the covers. For example, Karlův most has the reference 6C – indicating the grid square in which it is to be found.

Prices
An indication of the cost of restaurants and cafés at attractions is given by **£** signs: **£££** denotes higher prices, **££** denotes average prices, **£** denotes lower prices.

Hotel prices
Room per night: **£** budget (under 1,500Kč); **££** moderate (1,500–3,000Kč); **£££** expensive to luxury (over 3,000Kč)

Restaurant prices
Three-course meal per person without drinks: **£** budget (under 500Kč); **££** moderate (500–1,000Kč); **£££** expensive (over 1,000Kč)

Contents

The essence of...

It is easy to get to know Prague, even to feel at home here. To enjoy the city to the full, be prepared to abandon your sightseeing itinerary whenever the mood takes you – the galleries and museums can wait. Put away the map and wander off the beaten track. Don't neglect the side streets and courtyards, where Prague is often at its most beguiling. To see more, take the tram rather than the metro, and be prepared to go the extra mile: climb to the top of that hill – no city in Europe has more rewarding views.

features

Praguers know their minds and have always been willing – though not always able – to express them. Standing in Old Town Square, one is reminded of the great Czech religious reformer, Jan Hus, who took on the might of the Catholic Church in order to stand up for what he believed. As so often in the nation's history it was an unequal, albeit heroic, struggle. Over 500 years later, in January 1969, a university student, Jan Palach, suffered a horrific death by setting himself on fire rather than acquiesce in the Soviet invasion.

Politicians, of course, prefer to leave permanent monuments in brick and stone – the Klementinum, the Charles Bridge, the Wallenstein Palace, Obecní dům. Everywhere you walk in Prague, its buildings are reminders of the city's history; but they are also aesthetic statements by the architects, artists and sculptors who contributed so much to this most beautiful city. Prague is much more than a glorified museum, however; it is a dynamic place, where individuals are allowed, even encouraged, to stand out from the crowd. To take the city's pulse, spend time in the pubs and cafés that poke out of every nook and cranny. For the traditional view, head for U zlatého tygra (► 18), a spit and sawdust pub. But just as representative of today's Prague is Radost FX (► 133), a meeting place for young people from

around the world. Cosmopolitan and receptive to new ideas, Prague is now more irresistible than ever.

GEOGRAPHY

- Prague lies on the River Vltava at 50° 5′ north and 14° 25′ east – the heart of Central Europe. The lowest point is 176m (577ft) above sea level, the highest 396m (1,230ft). Prague is 292km (181 miles) from Vienna, 350km (217 miles) from Berlin, 1,037km (642 miles) from Paris and 1,377km (853 miles) from London.

POPULATION

- Prague covers an area of 497sq km (192 sq miles), about two-thirds that of New York, but its population is only 1,173,000, compared with New York City's 8 million. Fewer than 30,000 people (2.5 per cent) live in the historic core of the city; the overwhelming majority inhabit apartment blocks known as *paneláks*, on the outskirts. Some 95.5 per cent of the population is of Czech nationality.

TOURISM

- In 2004 approximately 7.5 million tourists visited the Czech Republic, mostly from Germany, America and Britain, although more and more Italians, Russians and Japanese are now visiting the country. Tourism makes up nearly 5 per cent of the country's GNP.

ENVIRONMENT FACTS AND FIGURES

Prague has:

- 10,000ha (24,710 acres) of green space
- 31km (19 miles) of rivers, 10 islands, 18 bridges
- 500,000 road vehicles
- 2,570km (1,593 miles) of road
- 43km (27 miles) of metro line with 43 stations.

food & drink

You can be sure of one thing when you eat out in Prague – or anywhere else in the Czech Republic, for that matter: you will not go hungry. All the national dishes are incredibly rich and filling.

MEAT AND VEG

Czech cuisine is heavily meat-based. Pork, beef and chicken are all standard fare – but the pig is king. Popular dishes include pork with dumplings and *sauerkraut* (pickled cabbage), roast duck with bacon dumplings, and roast beef with a sour cream sauce. *Wiener schnitzel*, known to the Czechs as *smažený řízek*, is another favourite. In expensive restaurants, you can buy game – venison, pheasant, hare or even wild boar. Most meat is boiled or roasted and served in gravy and accompanied by potatoes or dumplings *(knedlíky)*.

Fresh vegetables, other than the ubiquitous *sauerkraut*, are appearing on menus with increasing frequency. On nearly every menu you'll find *šopsky salát* – sometimes called *balkansky salát* – which is a small bowl of chopped olives, bell peppers and

cucumbers in a sweet vinegar with a salty white cheese shredded liberally on top. Most restaurants also offer several side dishes at the end of the menu: small plates of vegetables, pasta, potatoes or rice. Vegetarians should note that many apparently meatless dishes are cooked in animal fat. The best advice is to declare yourself at the outset: *Jsem vegetarian (-ka* for the feminine form). Or ask for a meal *bez maso* (without meat).

Of the fish dishes, boiled carp served in melted butter, roasted pike, fillet of trout cooked in a green pepper sauce and smoked salmon

are all delicious. Try to leave some room for a dessert such as apple strudel or plum dumplings.

BEER

Czech beer is justifiably famous and is fully appreciated by the Czechs themselves – the Republic boasts the highest *per capita* consumption in the world: 153.6 litres (34gal) annually. Plzeň produces the clear golden nectar known as Pilsner Urquell in Germany and locally as Plzeňský Prazdroj. Gambrinus is another common brand. The other main centre of beer production is the southern Bohemian town of České Budějovice, Budweis in German. Don't be misled by the name – the American beer, Budweiser, and

the Czech brew, Budvar, have nothing in common. These brews are delicious, but local beers like Staropramen and Braník are just as good. If you fancy trying a dark *(tmave)* beer, head for U Fleků (➤ 163), which produces its own brand. The generic term for beer is *pivo*.

WINES AND SPIRITS

Most Czech wine is produced in the warmer, more sheltered parts of southern Moravia and is consumed locally, rather than exported. The best of the red wines is Frankovka or Vavřinecké – Tramín is a reliable white variety. The Mělník region, just north of Prague, produces a small amount of wine of variable quality (sometimes none at all, if the weather is bad). A dry white wine known as Rulandské bílé is probably the best, and can often be found on menus. There are three types of liqueur worth sampling: Borovicka, a fiery, juniper-flavoured spirit with the impact of an Italian grappa, which should be treated with the same respect; Slivovice, a plum brandy and, best of all, the wonderfully aromatic Becherovka, a herb-based 'health' drink concocted in the 19th century by a doctor in the spa town of Karlovy Vary.

short break

If you have only a short time to visit Prague and would like to take home some unforgettable memories, you can do something local and capture the real flavour of the city. The following suggestions will give you a wide range of sights and experiences that won't take very long, won't cost very much and will make your visit very special. If you only have time to choose just one of these, you will have found the true heart of the city.

- **Listen to the buskers** (street musicians) on the Charles Bridge (► 89) throughout the day while browsing the many stalls for souvenirs or art.

• **Watch Christ and his Twelve Apostles** signal the hour as they emerge from the Astronomical Clock in Old Town Square (➤ 46). The first figure to emerge is that of a skeleton, representing Death, followed by the Twelve Apostles. The clock not only gives the time but also shows the signs of the zodiac and seasons as well as the course of the sun.

• **Go to see Kafka's house** in Golden Lane (➤ 129), in the grounds of Prague Castle (➤ 44–45). The famous scribe wrote some of his best works here in his sister's stone cottage tucked away within the castle walls. You can find reference to Golden Lane in Kafka's *The Castle.*

• **Take either tram 22 or 23** on its scenic journey through the Malá Strana and up to Hradčany. The tram runs from Vinohrady through Nové Město and then across the river to Malá Strana and ending at the Hradčany area.

• **Take a walk up Wenceslas Square** (➤ 52–53) stopping to look at Josef Myslbek's famous equestrian statue of St Wenceslas and the small shrine to the martyrs of the Communist era. St Wenceslas is flanked at the foot of the monument by statues of his grandmother Ludmila, Vojtěk, Prokop and Anežska (Agnes). The Square became the focus for demonstrating Praguers and has been the scene of both tragic and joyous events in the city's history – most recently, the Velvet Revolution of 1989, which drove out the Communist regime.

- **Visit U zlatého tygra** (Jilská 4, Staré Město), a traditional Czech pub, where guests sit at plain wooden tables and wait to be served glasses of the frothy Pilsner Urquell lager. Noted as one of the top three pubs in Prague, make sure you get there early as seats fill up quickly.

- **See the Picassos and Van Goghs** in the Veletrzny Palace (➤ 54–55). Built in 1928, this huge building has six floors all accessible by lift (elevator) and shows works by Picasso and other European artists.

- **Visit the wonderful art nouveau confection, Obecní dům** (➤ 155). Built as a civic centre in the 1900s, it has undergone complete renovation. The Smetana Hall on the first floor is the city's largest concert hall and is where the opening concert of the Prague Spring Music Festival is held each year.

- **Listen to some Mozart** – the real thing at the Estates Theatre (➤ 97) or starring puppets at the National Marionette Theatre (➤ 146). The

Estates Theatre hosted the première of Mozart's *Don Giovanni* in 1787 and this opera can still be seen here today or alternately performed by puppets at the National Marionette Theatre.

• **Enjoy the peaceful surroundings** of the Royal Gardens (➤ 116–117). They are accessed from the Powder Bridge to the north of the castle and were created by Ferdinand I in 1534 to include fountains and manicured lawns.

Planning

Before You Go

WHEN TO GO

JAN	FEB	MAR	APR	MAY	JUN	JUL	AUG	SEP	OCT	NOV	DEC
-1°C	0°C	4°C	9°C	14°C	17°C	19°C	18°C	14°C	9°C	4°C	0°C
30°F	32°F	39°F	48°F	57°F	63°F	66°F	65°F	57°F	48°F	39°F	32°F

High season Low season

Temperatures are the **average daily maximum** for each month.

Prague has hot summers and bitterly cold winters. May and June and then September and October are the best times to go, although Prague's winter snow can be great, with the concert and opera seasons at their height. Go in spring to see the wonderful show of blossoms on the fruit trees of Petřín Hill and avoid the oppressive heat of summer. However, January to March, and November are the best times to go if you want to avoid the hustle and bustle of tourist crowds.

Autumn is a lovely time to visit when the days are still bright with sunshine but the crowds have dwindled. Come in freezing winter to visit the markets and join the New Years' crowds in the streets.

WHAT YOU NEED

● Required
○ Suggested
▲ Not required

Some countries require a passport to remain valid for a minimum period (usually at least six months) beyond the date of entry – check before you travel.

	UK	Germany	USA	Netherlands	Spain
Passport/National Identity Card	●	●	●	●	●
Visa (Regulations can vary – check before you travel)	▲	▲	▲	▲	▲
Onward or Return Ticket	▲	▲	▲	▲	▲
Health Inoculations	▲	▲	▲	▲	▲
Health Documentation (➤ 23, Health Advice)	●	●	●	●	●
Travel Insurance	○	○	○	○	○
Driving Licence (national)	●	●	●	●	●
Car Insurance Certificate	●	●	●	●	●
Car Registration Document	●	●	●	●	●

ADVANCE PLANNING WEBSITES

- Prague Information Service: **www.**prague-info.cz
- City of Prague Official Guide: **www.**welcometoPrague.cz

TOURIST INFORMATION

In the UK

Czech Tourism Great Britain
13 Harley Street, London
W1G 9QG
☎ (020) 7631 0427;
brochure line ☎ (090) 6364 0641
www.czechtourism.com

In the USA

Czech Tourism USA, 1109–1111 Madison Avenue, New York, NY 10028 ☎ (212) 288 0830

In Canada

Czech Tourist Authority, 401 Bay Street, Suite 1510 Simpson Tower, Toronto, Ontario M5H 2Y4
☎ (416) 363 9928

In Australia

Czech Embassy, 8 Culgoa Circuit, O'Malley, ACT 2606, Canberra
☎ (02) 6290 1386

HEALTH ADVICE

Medical insurance

All visitors to the Czech Republic must carry health insurance to cover any medical services whilst in the country/ and or hospital fees and repatriation costs. EU Nationals may be eligible for additional medical care and should show their passport when seeking medical attention. US visitors should check their insurance coverage.

Dental services

Dental treatment must be paid for. Emergency 24-hour care is available at Palackého 5, Nové Město, Praha 1 ☎ 224 946 981.

TIME DIFFERENCES

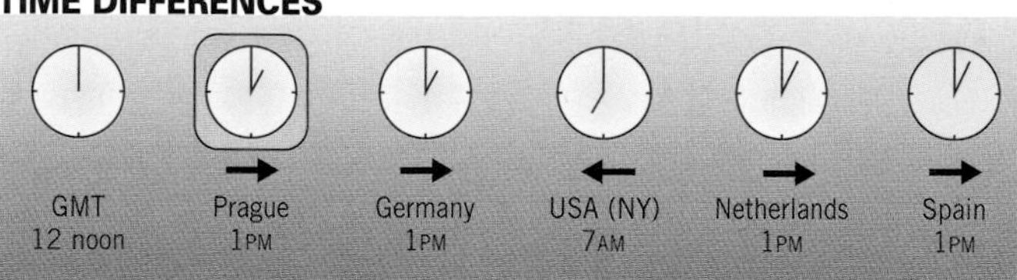

The Czech Republic is on Central European Time (GMT+1), but from late March, when clocks are put forward one hour, until late October, Czech Summer Time (GMT+2) operates.

WHAT'S ON WHEN

19 January *Jan Palach Day:* The country marks the day in 1969 when 20-year-old Charles University student Jan Palach died after setting fire to himself (on January 16) on Wenceslas Square to protest the invasion by Warsaw Pact troops the previous August,

and subsequent Soviet occupation of Czechoslovakia.

March *International Music Festival:* A series of classical and contemporary concerts is performed in venues all over the city throughout the month.

30 April *Witches' Night:* A bonfire held on Petřín Hill celebrates the traditional end of winter and the birth of spring.

Early May *Prague Spring:* A three-week event of classical music and dance, performed in churches, palaces and concert halls around Prague. The celebrations begin with a procession from Smetana's grave in Vyšehrad to his namesake concert hall in Obecní dům.

First week of June *Fringe Theatre Festival Prague:* This is a week of indoor and outdoor performances around the city by drama, music, comedy and dance troupes.

Late August *Festival of Italian Operas:* Puccini, Verdi and Rossini top the bill during this 10-day festival at the State Opera House.

Mid-September *Prague Autumn Music Festival:* Three weeks of classical music performances by orchestras and musicians from around the world.

Late September *Vinohrady Grape Harvest:* An annual celebration of the country's first grape harvest takes place in two main squares in the neighbourhood that was home to the Royal Vineyards during

NATIONAL HOLIDAYS

JAN	FEB	MAR	APR	MAY	JUN	JUL	AUG	SEP	OCT	NOV	DEC
1		(1)	(1)	2		2			1		3

1 Jan	New Year's Day	**6 Jul**	Jan Hus Day
Mar/Apr	Easter Monday	**28 Sep**	Czech Statehood Day
1 May	May Day	**28 Oct**	Independence Day
8 May	Liberation Day	**17 Nov**	Democracy Day
May/Jun	Whit Sunday and Monday	**24–25 Dec**	Christmas Eve/Day
5 Jul	St Cyril and St Method Day	**26 Dec**	St Stephen's Day

Restaurants, museums and other tourist attractions tend to stay open on these days.

Charles IV's reign. Traditional music and crafts along with plenty of *burčak* – the sweet but potent young wine.

Late October *International Jazz Festival:* For almost 30 years Prague has hosted this week-long festival of performances by jazz legends from the United States to Ukraine, with plenty of local stars in between.

17 November *Anniversary of the Velvet Revolution:* A commemoration and wreath-laying ceremony conducted on Wenceslas Square and Národní (although there has been much concern voiced by citizens recently about the poor attendance at this event).

December *Christmas market on Old Town Square:* Every festive season a giant Christmas tree lights up the centre of the square, while the space around it is crammed with market stalls selling carved toys, bobbin lace, ceramics, glass figurines, Christmas ornaments and tasty gingerbread cakes, barbecued sausages and *svarak* (mulled wine). Entertainment is provided by street performers.

Getting There

AIR

Prague's international airport is **Ruzyně Airport** (☎ 220 113 314) which has all the modern amenities you would expect of a European airport.

Czech Airlines – ČSA (☎ 239 007 007; **www.**csa.cz) operates direct scheduled flights to Prague from Britain, mainland Europe and North America. Flight time from London is 2 hours. Prague is connected by rail to all main European capitals (► 28, Getting Around). Other international carriers that fly into Prague include British Airways, Alitalia, KLM, Lufthansa, SAS and Air France.

Ruzyně Airport is 20km (12 miles) from the city centre and a 20- to 40-minute journey depending on your mode of transport.

Airport taxis are expensive, but AAA taxis are reasonably priced and have English-speaking operators (☎ 14014).

The next best method into town is on a **Cedaz minibus** (☎ 220 114 296) which run every 30 minutes between 5.30am and 9.30pm and will drop you at the Náměstí Republiky for around 90Kč per person. Cedaz will also take you or your whole party to your hotel for a reasonable set charge of a few hundred crowns. Look for the booth signed 'City Centre 90Kc'.

If you don't have a lot of luggage take the No 119 bus from the airport to Dejvická metro station. From there, take the main A-line into any of the four city-centre stations. This service runs every day from 5am–midnight, as do the buses.

RAIL

The overnight train from London – via Brussels and Cologne (information: ☎ 221 111 122; **www.**cdrail.cz) arrives at **Hlavní nádraží** which is on the 'C' (red) metro line. Inside the train station there is a tourist information office, ATM machines, exchange facilities and a 24-hour left-luggage office. It is a short walk from **Václavské náměstí** (Wenceslas Square). Some international trains also arrive at Prague's other main station **Nádraží Holešovice.** Several trams run along the park in front of the station.

BUS

International and national bus services arrive at **Florenc** bus and metro station on the east side of the city. The Old Town is then just a 5-minute walk or the B and C metro lines next door can take you anywhere else you want to go.

DRIVING

Driving is on the right.
Speed limit on motorways (annual toll payable):
130kph (80mph)
Minimum limit:
50kph (31mph)
Speed limit on country roads:
90kph (56mph) (on level crossings: **30kph/18mph)**
Speed limit on urban roads:
50kph (31mph)
Seat belts must be worn in front seats – and rear seats where fitted. Under 12s may not travel in the front seat.

Drink driving *Don't* drink *any* alcohol if driving. The allowed blood/alcohol level is zero and penalties are severe.

Fuel Petrol *(benzín)* is sold in leaded form as *special* (91 octane) and *super* (96 octane). Unleaded petrol comes as *natural* (95 octane) and *super plus* (98 octane); the latter is available only at larger petrol stations. Diesel *(nafta)* is also available. In Prague, filling stations are few and far between, but some open 24 hours.

If you break down, ÚAMK, the Czech automobile club, operates a 24-hour nationwide breakdown service on the same terms as your own motoring club at home (non-members pay in full), ☎ 0123 (123 in Prague) or 154 from mobile phones. On motorways use emergency phones (every 2km/1 mile) to summon help.

Getting Around

TRANSPORTATION

Internal Flights Czech Airlines (ČSA ✉ V celnici 5, Praha 1 ☎ 239 007 007; **www.**csa.cz) and a variety of other carriers link Prague with Brno and Ostrava. Though not cheap, especially when compared with the train or bus, they are useful when you want to get somewhere quickly.

Trains Czech Railways (České Dráhy ☎ 221 111 122, 24-hours; **www.**cd.cz) run *rychlík* that stop only at major towns and *osobní* calling at every station. International trains to destinations outside the country leave from the main station Hlavní nádraží. Services to north and east Bohemia depart from Masarykovo nádraží; routes to the south are from Smíchovské nádraží.

River boats From April to September cruise boats ply the Vltava River, as far as Troja Château in the north of Prague and Slapy Lake in the south. The Prague Steamship Company (Pražská paroplavební společnost ☎ 2493 00 017; **www.**paroplavba.cz) is the main operator. There are usually boats tied up along the riverbank.

Metro Prague's metro is clean, fast and cheap. There are three lines: A (green), B (yellow) and C (red). Trains run 5am to midnight, every 2 minutes peak times (5 to 10 minutes other times). The letter 'M' with a downward arrow marks a station entrance. For information (also trams and buses) see **www.**dp-praha.cz/en/.

Trams/buses After the metro, trams *(tramvaj)* are the fastest way of getting around. There are 26 lines running every 6 to 8 minutes at peak times (10 to 15 minutes other times). Buses *(autobusy)* mainly keep out of the centre. There is one ticket for the metro, tram and bus. Tickets are available at *tabaks*, newspaper kiosks, metro stations and some tram stops (look for the yellow machine), and cost 14Kč single, 10Kč child. Multi-day passes are also available (3 days: 220Kč, 7 days: 280Kč, 15 days: 320Kč). Failure to produce a valid ticket on request will result in a 800Kč fine (400Kč on the spot).

DRIVING

A car is not necessary or advised in Prague as much of the city is off-limits to cars and parking is by permit only. If you're heading out of town, car rental is easy to arrange, but can be expensive. Shop around as some local firms charge less than well-known names. Try Dvořák Rent-a-Car (☎ 224 926 260) or Europcar (☎ 224 811 290).

TAXIS

Taxis abound in Prague. An unoccupied taxi has a lit-up sign and may be hailed on the street or hired from a taxi rank. Registered taxis should have a meter clearly displayed. Look for AAA, ProfiTaxi and City Taxi. You have the right to a printed receipt.

The Prague Card This three-day tourist pass provides entry to Prague Castle, all the city's major museums and historic buildings and for a bit more, unlimited travel on the metro, trams and bus. Adult card with transportation is 810Kč, or 590Kč without. Buy cards at Prague Information Service Offices at Staroměstská radnice, Hlavní nádraží station or Malostranská Mostecká vez (► 30). For further information, see **www.**pis.cz/en.

CONCESSIONS

Students/youths Holders of an International Student Identity Card (ISIC) are entitled to a 50 per cent reduction on admission to Prague's museums. Student cards also offer reductions on international trains, though not on domestic public transport. GTS (✉ Ve Smečkách 33, Praha 1 ☎ 222 211 204) specializes in travel for students and independent travellers.

Senior citizens There are no special senior citizen concessions. However, Saga Holidays organize holidays for over 50s and have trips to Prague (✉ Middelburg Square, Folkestone CT20 1AZ, UK ☎ 0800 414 383; **www.**saga.co.uk).

Being There

TOURIST OFFICES

Czech Tourist Authority
(Česká centrála cestovního ruchu)
✉ Vinohradská 46, 12041 Praha 2
☎ 221 580 111
www.czechtourism.com

Prague Information Service
(Pražská informační služba PIS)
✉ Staroměstská radnice (Old Town Hall), Staroměstské náměstí, Praha 1
☎ 224 482 202
www.prague-info.cz
Mon–Fri 8–7
Staroměstská

✉ Hlavní nádraží (Main Railway Sation) Wilsonova, Praha 1
Apr–Oct Mon–Fri 9–7, Sat–Sun 9–4; Nov–Mar Mon–Fri 9–6, Sat–Sun 9–3
Hlavní nádraží

✉ Malostranská Mostecká vez, (Lesser Town Tower), Mostecká, Praha 1
Apr–Oct daily 10–6
Malostranská

Prague Tourist Centre
✉ Celetná 14, Karlova 1, Národní 4, Nerudova 4 (all Praha 1)
www.aroundprague.cz
Daily 9–8
Staroměstská

EMBASSIES AND CONSULATES

UK ☎ 257 402 111
Germany ☎ 257 531 481
USA ☎ 257 530 663
Netherlands ☎ 233 015 200
Spain ☎ 233 097 211

TELEPHONES

There are public telephones on the street and near metro stations. Local calls cost 4Kč and can only be made from

OPENING HOURS

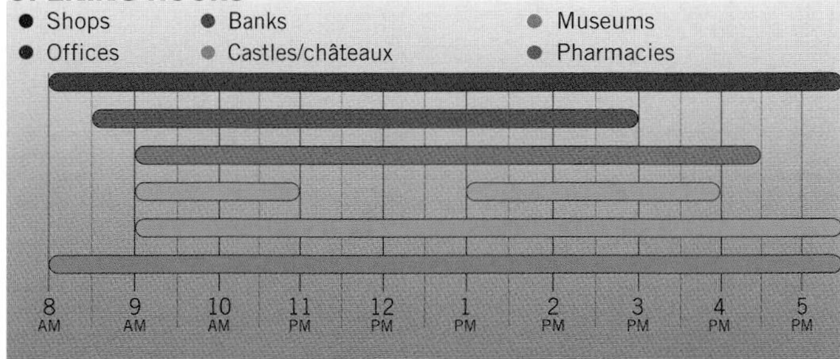

Some shops close for lunch but most open all day. On weekends, usual hours are Sat 10–7 and Sun 10–5. Grocery stores *(potraviny)* open from 7am; department stores and large shopping centres open until 8pm or 9pm. Outside Prague centre, shops are usually closed on Sunday except for malls in the suburbs. Some pharmacies open 24 hours. Banks vary, some open Saturday morning. Museums and art galleries usually open from 10–6; they are closed Mondays. Castles, châteaux and other historical monuments open daily (except Monday) May to September and weekends in April and October, but may be closed other times; please check.

---

the old orange phones which accept only 1Kč coins. Grey phones take 1, 2, 5 and 10Kč coins. There are also phonecard *(telefonní karta)* booths. Buy cards (200 and 300Kč) from post offices, *tabaks*, grocery stores and newsagents. Country code: 42, Prague city code: 02.

INTERNATIONAL DIALLING CODES

From Czech Republic to:
UK: 00 44
Germany: 00 49
USA: 00 1
Netherlands: 00 31
Spain: 00 34

EMERGENCY TELEPHONE NUMBERS

Police:
☎ 112 or 158
Ambulance:
☎ 112 or 155
Fire:
☎ 112 or 150

POSTAL SERVICES

Post offices

Post offices have distinctive orange *Pošta* signs. The main post office (✉ Jindřišská 14, Nové Město, Praha 1) is open daily 24 hours. There are several branches in the city which are open 8am–7pm (noon Sat) and closed Sun (☎ 221 131 445, non-English speaker).

ELECTRICITY

The power supply in the Czech Republic is 220 volts. Plugs are of the two-round-pin variety, so an adaptor is needed for most non-Continental European appliances and a voltage transformer for appliances operating on 100–120 volts.

CURRENCY AND FOREIGN EXCHANGE

The monetary unit of the Czech Republic is the Koruna česká (Kč) – or Czech crown – which is divided into 100 haléř – or heller. There are coins of 10, 20 and 50 hellers and 1, 2, 5, 10, 20 and 50 crowns. Banknotes come in 20, 50, 100, 200, 500, 1,000 and 5,000 crowns. Money may be changed at the airport, in banks (➤ 31, Opening Hours), major hotels, Čedok offices, and in the centre of Prague at exchange offices. Exchange offices advertising 'No Commission' are usually a poor place to change money and the no commission policy only applies if you're changing large amounts of money.

TIPS/GRATUITIES

Yes ✓ No ✕		
Hotels	✕	
Restaurants	✓	10%
Cafés/bars	✓	10%
Taxis	✓	10%
Tour guides	✓	20Kč
Porters	✓	40Kč
Hairdressers	✓	10%
Cloakroom attendants	✓	2Kč
Theatre/cinema usherettes	✕	
Toilets	✓	2Kč

HEALTH AND SAFETY

Sun advice The sun is not a real problem in Prague. June to August is the sunniest (and hottest) period but there are often thunder showers to cool things down. If the summer sun is fierce, apply a sunscreen and wear a hat, or visit a museum.

Drugs Pharmacies *(lékárna* or *apothéka)* are the only places to sell over-the-counter medicines. They also dispense many drugs *(leky)* normally available only by prescription in other Western countries.

Safe water Tap water is perfectly safe but heavily chlorinated so it can have a metallic taste. Bottled water is available everywhere: *né perlivá* is still water, *jemně perlivá* is lightly carbonated and *perlivá* is carbonated.

Personal safety Prague is a comparatively safe city, though petty crime is on the increase in central areas. Report any loss or theft to the *městská policie* (municipal police) – black uniforms.

- Watch your bag in tourist areas, and on the metro/trams, especially trams 22 and 23.
- Deposit your passport and valuables in the hotel safe.
- Never leave valuables in your car.

CLOTHING SIZES

Czech Republic	UK	Rest of Europe	USA	
46	36	46	36	
48	38	48	38	
50	40	50	40	
52	42	52	42	
54	44	54	44	Suits
56	46	56	46	
41	7	41	8	
42	7.5	42	8.5	
43	8.5	43	9.5	
44	9.5	44	10.5	
45	10.5	45	11.5	Shoes
46	11	46	12	
37	14.5	37	14.5	
38	15	38	15	
39/40	15.5	39/40	15.5	
41	16	41	16	
42	16.5	42	16.5	Shirts
43	17	43	17	
34	8	34	6	
36	10	36	8	
38	12	38	10	
40	14	40	12	
42	16	42	14	Dresses
44	18	44	16	
38	4.5	38	6	
38	5	38	6.5	
39	5.5	39	7	
39	6	39	7.5	
40	6.5	40	8	Shoes
41	7	41	8.5	

Best places to see

1 Chrám svatého Mikuláš (St Nicholas's Church)

www.psalterium.cz

The all-powerful Jesuit Order commissioned this superb church, the ultimate expression of Prague baroque, at the beginning of the 18th century.

Restored at a cost of 120 million Czech crowns, this monumental building was constructed between 1704 and 1756 by father-and-son team,

Christoph and Kilián Dientzenhofer, and completed by Kilián's son-in-law, Anselmo Lurago. The interior decoration builds on an accumulation of *trompe l'oeil* effects, culminating in *The Apotheosis of St Nicholas* by Johann Kracker, a fresco covering more than 1,500sq m (1,795sq yds) of the nave ceiling. The splendid dome is 18m (59ft) higher than the Petřín Tower. But not everything is as costly as it appears. Many of the mottled pink and green pillars and other details are *faux marbre*, while the four more than life-size statues under the dome are made of wood, with a surface covering of glazed chalk. These dramatic characterizations of the Church Fathers include a vigorous St Cyril triumphantly lancing the devil with his crozier. The sculptor, Ignaz Platzer, also created the copper statue of St Nicholas, which looks down from the high altar. Also of note is the rococo pulpit, overhanging with angels and cherubs, which was made by Peter and Richard Práchner in 1765. The baroque organ, played by Mozart in 1787, boasts 2,500 pipes and 44 registers. Four years later it was played at a funeral Mass in his memory. The church was full to overflowing, evidence of the esteem in which he was held here.

4C Malostranské náměstí, Malá Strana, Praha 1 Mar–Oct daily 9–5; Nov–Feb daily 9–4. Concerts Wed–Mon at 6pm Inexpensive Cafés (£), restaurants (££–£££) near by Malostranská 12, 20, 22, 23

2 Josefov

www.jewishmuseum.cz

For more than 700 years this attractive neighbourhood of the Old Town has been home to Prague's Jewish community.

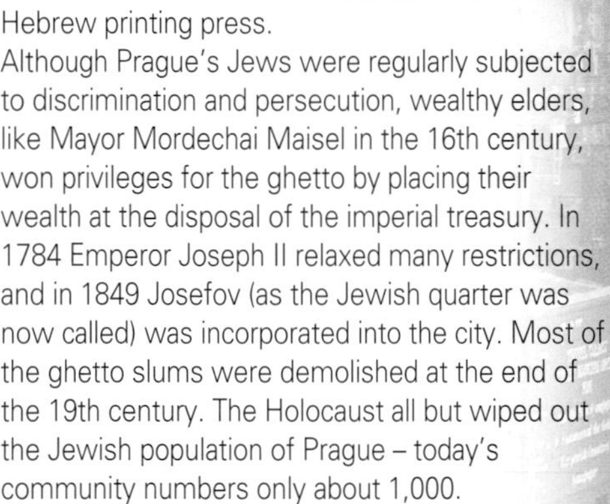

Jewish people first settled in the Old Town in the 12th century. In 1254 the area was surrounded by a ghetto wall, following a decree of the third Lateran Council. The ghetto was a centre of learning, with its own Talmudic school and Hebrew printing press. Although Prague's Jews were regularly subjected to discrimination and persecution, wealthy elders, like Mayor Mordechai Maisel in the 16th century, won privileges for the ghetto by placing their wealth at the disposal of the imperial treasury. In 1784 Emperor Joseph II relaxed many restrictions, and in 1849 Josefov (as the Jewish quarter was now called) was incorporated into the city. Most of the ghetto slums were demolished at the end of the 19th century. The Holocaust all but wiped out the Jewish population of Prague – today's community numbers only about 1,000.

Hitler planned a museum in Josefov recording the history of the 'extinct' Jewish race. Ironically, this ensured the preservation of treasures and furnishings confiscated from synagogues all over

Bohemia and Moravia. They are now exhibited in three of the restored synagogues. The Pinkas Synagogue is a particularly poignant Holocaust memorial. Also in Josefov are the Old Jewish Cemetery and the oldest synagogue in Europe: the Old-New Synagogue, which has been the focus of religious worship since the 13th century. The Jewish Town Hall, dating from 1763, is a baroque building with a distinctive green steeple. Set in one of the gables is a clock with hands that travel anti-clockwise, following the Hebrew lettering, which is read from right to left.

8C U Staré Školy 1, Josefov, Praha 1 222 317 191 Apr–Oct Sun–Fri 9–6; Nov–Mar Sun–Fri 9–4.30. Closed Jewish hols Moderate. Jewish Museum ticket includes most synagogues, the cemetery and Ceremonial Hall Staroměstská 17, 18

3 Katedrála svatého Víta (St Vitus's Cathedral)

www.hrad.cz

St Vitus's took nearly six centuries to complete and was consecrated only in 1929, yet it stands on the site of a chapel founded in 925.

Work started on the present Gothic building in 1344, under the direction of Matthias of Arras. German Petr Parléř and his two sons were responsible for the lofty choir and the surrounding chapels, which were finally completed early in the 15th century. The tower on the south side was given its Renaissance steeple in 1562, to which baroque embellishments were later added. The nave and the impressive west end date from the second half of the 19th century. The Golden Portal (the original entrance) on the south side contains a mosaic of the Last Judgement, dating from 1370, which has been restored to its former glory.

The Chapel of St Wenceslas, dating from 1358 to 1367, is one of the oldest parts of the building and the most beautifully decorated. The lower walls are encrusted with scintillating jasper and amethyst, while the frescoes (14th–16th centuries) depict scenes from the passion of Christ and the life of St Wenceslas (the saint is buried directly underneath the chapel). The foundations of the 11th-century Romanesque basilica were unearthed as the cathedral was nearing completion and can be seen in the crypt, along with the sarcophagi of the kings of Bohemia. King Vladislav Jagiello commissioned the beautiful Royal Oratory in the 1480s: the vaulted ceiling, shaped like the branches of a tree, is highly unusual. An exquisite silver funerary monument to the cult saint, John of Nepomuk, was erected in the choir in 1736. One of the cherubs points to the saint's tongue, which was said never to have decayed. The cathedral also contains fine 20th-century stained glass, notably Alphonse Mucha's portrait of saints Cyril and Methodius in the third chapel from the west end.

4D Pražský hrad, Hradčany, Praha 1 None Apr–Oct daily 9–5; Nov–Mar daily 9–4 Free; moderate charge for crypt, tower and choir Café (£), restaurants (££–£££) near by Malostranská 22, 23 to Pražský hrad

4 Loreta

www.loreta.cz

This pretty baroque shrine has been a place of pilgrimage since 1626, when it was endowed by a Bohemian noblewoman, Kateřina of Lobkowicz.

The Loreta shrine was inspired by a medieval legend. In 1278, so the story goes, the Virgin Mary's house in Nazareth was miraculously transported by angels to Loreto in Italy and thus saved from the Infidel. The Marian cult became an important propaganda weapon of the Counter-Reformation and, following the defeat of the Protestants at the Battle of the White Mountain in 1620, some 50 other Loreto shrines were founded in Bohemia and Moravia.

The heart of the Loreta is the Santa Casa, a replica of the Virgin's relocated house. Sumptuously decorated, it incorporates a beam and several bricks from the Italian original. On the

silver altar (behind a grille) is a small ebony statue of the Virgin. The rich stucco reliefs, depicting scenes from the lives of the prophets, are by Italian artists.

The much larger Church of the Nativity was designed by Kilián Dientzenhofer between 1734 and 1735, with ceiling frescoes by Václav Reiner and Johann Schöpf. Less edifying are the gruesome remains of saints Felecissimus and Marcia, complete with wax death masks. The cloisters, originally 17th century but with an upper storey added by Dientzenhofer in the 1740s, once provided overnight shelter for pilgrims. In the corner chapel of Our Lady of Sorrows is a diverting painting of St Starosta, a bearded lady who prayed for facial hair to put off an unwanted suitor, only to be crucified by her father whose plans for her wedding were thwarted. The Loreta treasury has a famed collection of vestments and other religious objects, including a diamond monstrance made in Vienna in 1699, which glitters with 6,200 precious stones.

2C Loretánské náměstí 7, Hradčany, Praha 1 220 516 740 Tue–Sun 9–12.15, 1–4.30 Inexpensive 22, 23

5 Pražský hrad (Prague Castle)

www.hrad.cz

Dominating Hradčany with majestic assurance, Prague Castle has a history stretching back more than a thousand years and is still the Czech State's administrative centre.

The Castle's château-like appearance dates from 1753 to 1775, when the Empress of Austria, Maria-Theresa, ordered its reconstruction, but the Gothic towers and spires of St Vitus's Cathedral are clues to a much older history. Many misfortunes took their toll on the churches and palaces, culminating in a disastrous fire in 1541 which engulfed the whole of Hradčany. Architecturally this was a blessing in disguise and the extensive restoration work resulted in the stunning Renaissance and baroque interiors of today's Royal Palace.

Entry to the Castle is through a series of enclosed courtyards. In the first, the changing of the guard takes place hourly in the shadow of huge baroque sculptures of battling Titans. The entrance to the second courtyard is through the Matthias Gate, which dates from 1614. Directly opposite is the 19th-century Chapel of the Cross, now the Information Centre. On the other side of the courtyard, the Picture Gallery of Prague Castle contains paintings from the Imperial collections, including minor works by Titian, Tintoretto, Veronese and Rubens. The third courtyard is dominated by St Vitus's Cathedral (➤ 40–41). To

the right, the 18th-century façade of the Royal Palace conceals a network of halls and chambers on various levels, dating from the Romanesque period onwards. The centrepiece is the magnificent Vladislav Hall. To the right are the former offices of the Chancellery of Bohemia, dating from the early 16th century, where, on 23 May 1618, after learning of the accession to the throne of the detested Archduke Ferdinand of Habsburg, more than 100 Protestant noblemen burst into the far room and threw two Catholic governors and a secretary out of the window. The officials survived the fall but the incident, known as the Defenestration of Prague, marked the start of the Thirty Years' War. The Diet Hall next door was designed by the Renaissance architect Bonifaz Wohlmut in 1563 and its walls are hung with portraits of the Habsburgs. The Riders' Staircase leads down to the remains of the Romanesque and Gothic Palaces and an exhibition on the castle.

The Castle complex's other outstanding monument is St George's Basilica (➤ 113) and a short walk away is the Lobkowicz Palace. Beyond Golden Lane, the Daliborka Tower is named after a nobleman imprisoned here on suspicion of complicity in a peasants' revolt. In the Mihulka, or Powder Tower, alchemists were once employed to elicit the secret of turning base metals into gold.

4D Hradčany, Praha 1 224 373 368 Apr–Oct daily 9–5; Nov–Mar daily 9–4 Moderate Cafés (£), restaurants (££–£££) 22, 23 Changing of the guard every hour on the hour at the main gate. Information centre in the third courtyard.

6 Staroměstská radnice (Old Town Hall)

www.pis.cz

The star attraction of Prague's most famous landmark is the enchanting Astronomical Clock.

The Old Town Hall is actually a row of houses adapted over the centuries by the council. In 1338 the burghers enlarged the merchant Volflin's house, and the tower and chapel were added in 1381. Neighbouring Kříž House was acquired in 1387. The house of furrier Mikš was added in 1548 and the house At the Cock in the 19th century.

The main attraction is the Astronomical Clock, which gives the time of day, the months and seasons of the year, the signs of the zodiac, the course of the sun and the holidays of the Christian calendar. On the hour, the figure of Death rings a bell and the 12 Apostles appear above. A cock crows and time is up for the Turk, who shakes his head in disbelief; the Miser, who eyes his bag of gold; and Vanity, who admires himself in a mirror.

Inside are the council chamber where Bohemian kings were elected, and a chapel with a distinctive oriel window. Climb the clock tower for views across the red rooftops of the city.

9C Staroměstské náměstí 1, Staré Město, Praha 1 236 002 562 8 Feb–Oct Mon 11–6, Tue–Sun 9–6; Nov–7 Feb Mon 11–5, Tue–Sun 9–5 Moderate Cafés (££), restaurants (£££) near by Staroměstská 17, 18 Tourist information office open all year.

7 Šternberský palác (Sternberg Palace)

www.ngprague.cz

The 17th-century baroque palace, built for Count Wenceslas Sternberg from 1698 to 1707, now houses the National Gallery's impressive collection of Old Masters.

The palace is set back from Hradčany Square (➤ 111): access is through the left-hand entrance of the Archbishop's Palace. The exhibition is

arranged chronologically by the artists' country of origin. The gallery's proudest possession is Albrecht Dürer's *Feast of the Rose Garlands* (1506), acquired by Emperor Rudolph II because it features one of his ancestors, Maximilian I (shown in the foreground with Pope Julius II). German painting is also represented by Holbein the Elder and Lucas Cranach, including a charming *Adam and Eve*. There are works by Geertgen tot Sint Jans, Jan Gossaert and the Brueghels, father and son. Pieter Brueghel the Elder's animated calendar painting, *The Haymaking* has a rhythmic, almost dance-like quality. Outstanding among the later work is a portrait by Rembrandt, *Scholar in his Study* (1634), and several paintings by Rubens, including *Martyrdom of St Thomas* (1637–39), which was commissioned for the church in Malá Strana. By comparison, the Italian Renaissance is less well represented, although Andrea della Robbia, Sebastiano del Piombo and Pietro della Francesca all feature in the collection and there are some fine altar panels by the 14th-century Sienese artist, Pietro Lorenzetti. Paintings by artists of the 18th-century Venetian school, including Tiepolo and Canaletto, and two fine Spanish works, El Greco's *Head of Christ* and a portrait by Goya of Don Miguel de Lardizabal, can also be found in the gallery. The superb collection of 19th- and 20th-century French art is now in the Veletrzny Palace (➤ 54–55).

3D Hradčanské náměstí 15, Hradčany, Praha 1 220 514 634 Tue–Sun 10–6 Inexpenive; free first Wed of the month Café (££) Malostranská 22, 23 to Pražský hrad

8 Strahovský klášter (Strahov Monastery)

www.strahovskyklaster.cz

Strahovní means 'watching over', and this ancient religious foundation, famous as a centre of learning, has been guarding the western approaches to Hradčany since the 12th century.

Above the baroque gateway is a statue of the founder of the Premonstratensian Order, St Norbert; to the left of the gate is the Church of St Roch, patron saint of plague victims, commissioned by Rudolf II in 1603 after Prague had narrowly escaped an epidemic. It is now used for modern art exhibitions. The twin-towered Abbey Church of the Nativity has a Romanesque core, but its present appearance dates from around 1750, when Anselmo Lurago remodelled the western façade. Mozart played the organ here on two occasions. The vaulted ceiling is sumptuously decorated with cartouches and frescoes by Jiří Neunhertz, depicting the legend of St Norbert, whose remains were brought here from Magdeburg in 1627 and reburied in the chapel of St Ursula, on the left of the nave.

The library of the Strahov Monastery is more than 800 years old and among the

finest in Europe. The Theological Hall, built between 1671 and 1679 by Giovanni Orsi, has walls lined with elaborately carved bookcases, stacked with precious volumes and manuscripts. The Philosophical Hall dates from 1782 to 1784, and its entire ceiling is covered with a delightful composition entitled *The Spiritual Development of Mankind*, by Franz Maulbertsch. The library contains over 130,000 volumes, including 2,500 books published before 1500, and 3,000 manuscripts. The oldest book, the 9th-century *Strahov Gospels*, is on show in the entrance.

1B Strahovské nádvoří 1/132, Hradčany, Praha 1
233 107 718 Library: daily 9–noon, 1–5; Gallery: 9–noon, 12.30–5. Closed Christmas and Easter
Moderate Restaurant (££) 22, 23 to Pohořelec

9 Václavské náměstí (Wenceslas Square)

Wenceslas Square really comes alive after dark, when its restaurants, cinemas and nightclubs attract a boisterous crowd.

Prague's most famous thoroughfare is actually an impressive 750m-long (898yd) boulevard, dominated at the northern end by Josef Schulz's neo-Renaissance National Museum (➤ 154). Once staging a horse market, Wenceslas Square was

later a focus for political demonstration. When the Soviet army occupied Prague in August 1968 it was here that the distraught population gathered to protest. Several months later a student, Jan Palach, burned himself to death on the steps of the National Museum. Following the collapse of the Communist regime in December 1989, Václav Havel and Alexander Dubcek appeared on the balcony of No 36 to greet their ecstatic supporters. Palach and other victims of the regime are commemorated in a small shrine in front of Josef Myslbek's equestrian statue of St Wenceslas.

Wenceslas Square became a showcase for modern Czech architecture when the traditional two- and three-storey baroque houses were demolished in the 19th century. The neo-Renaissance Wiehl House was completed in 1896 and is decorated with florid sgraffito and statuary by Mikuláš Aleš. Many of the sumptuous art nouveau interiors and fittings in the Europa Hotel (No 25) have survived and are also worth investigating. The functionalist Koruna palác (No 1), a covered shopping arcade with a stunning glass dome dating from 1911, became the model for other passageways linking the square with the neighbouring streets (the Lucerna, at No 61, was built by Václav Havel's grandfather). The former insurance offices on the corner of Jindřišská could well have been the stuff of nightmares for Franz Kafka when he worked here as a clerk from 1906 to 1907.

10A Václavské náměstí, Nové Město, Praha 1
Free Můstek, Muzeum 3, 9, 14

10 Veletržní palác (Veletrzny Palace)

www.ngprague.cz

The gallery's outstanding collection of modern Czech and European art is housed in a 1920s constructivist palace.

Designed by Oldřich Tyl and Josef Fuchs for the Prague Trade Fair of 1928, the enormous glass-fronted building was described by the famous modernist architect, Le Corbusier, as 'breathtaking'. The priceless French collection runs the gamut of Impressionist and post-Impressionist artists. Among the highlights are *Two Women among the Flowers* by Monet (1875), *Green Rye* by Van Gogh (1889), and one of Gauguin's Tahiti paintings, *Flight*

(1902). Picasso is represented by several contrasting paintings, ranging from an arresting, primitivist *Self Portrait*, dating from 1907, to *Clarinet* (1911), a classic example of analytic Cubism. There are also works by Braque, Chagall, Derain, Vlaminck, Raoul Dufy, Fernand Léger, Albert Marquet and Marie Laurencin. Among the sculptures are works by Rodin, Henri Laurens and an unusual study of a dancer by Dégas.

French painting was a major source of inspiration for Czech artists seeking an alternative to the predominant German culture of the late 19th century. Jan Zrzavy, Bohumil Kubišta and Emil Filla all progressed from neo-Impressionism to more abstract styles. Kubišta's *Still Life with Funnel* (1910) was directly influenced by a similar study by Picasso. Other artists producing Cubist works at the time include Filla, Václav Špála and the sculptor Otto Gutfreund. The Czechs' affinity with French art becomes even more noticeable in the inter-war period, when the two countries were closely bound together by political and diplomatic ties. The crowning moment came in 1935, when the founder of the Surrealist movement, André Breton, visited Czechoslovakia at the invitation of the Prague Surrealists, Jindřich Štyrský, Vincenc Makovsky and Toyen (Marie Čermínová). The exhibition concludes with sections on post-war and contemporary art.

28P Dukelských hrdinů 47, Holešovice, Praha 7 224 301 024 Tue–Sun 10–6 Moderate Restaurant (££); internet café (£) Vltavská 5, 12, 17 to Veletržni Holešovice

Best things to do

Ways to be a local

A good sense of humour and a sense of the ridiculous are typical Czech characteristics, so be ready to share a joke.

Sample the atmosphere in a traditional pub *(pivnice /hospoda)*, like U zlatého tygra (► 18).

Check out the form at the races; with hurdle, steeplechases and trotting ✉ Velká Chuchle course, Radotínská 69, Praha 5 ☎ 257 941 042; www.velka-chuchle.cz

It's polite to share a table in a crowded restaurant and a good way to get to know Czechs.

Take a short cut through the passageways off Wenceslas Square (► 52–53).

Learn a few words of Czech. More Praguers are coming to terms with English, but they'll appreciate your efforts: *dobry den* (hello), *prosim* (please), *děkuje* (thank you).

If you're invited into a Czech home, take some flowers for your hosts and take your shoes off inside the door.

Don't talk about communism or the Russians. Many Czechs prefer to forget the occupation. A safer topic of conversation is the much-loved First Republic (the inter-war years).

Enjoy a fast-food lunch in the Franciscan Gardens.

Go and watch Prague's leading soccer and ice hockey teams (both called Sparta Praha) at a home game. You can buy their colours from department stores.

Places to have lunch

Byblos

Lebanese and Middle Eastern dishes served in an airy, plant-filled restaurant in the city's stock-exchange hall.

✉ Burzovni palác, Rybná 14, Staré Město ☎ 221 842 121; www.biblos.cz

Café Louvre

Upstairs restaurant (non-smoking room) with views of the art nouveau architecture on Národní.

✉ Národní třída 20, Nové Město ☎ 224 930 949; www.cafelouvre.cz

Kavána Slavia

Captivating views of the river and Malá Strana make this art deco café-restaurant special.

✉ Corner of Smetanovo nábřeži and Národní, Staré Město ☎ 224 239 604

Klub architektů

A multi-roomed 14th-century cellar restaurant with excellent

cooking from a chef who brings a Mediterranean and Asian influence to traditional Czech dishes. Reservations recommended for dinner.

✉ Betlémské náměstí 5A, Staré Město ☎ 224 401 214

Nebožížek Restaurant

The food isn't special but the views from the terrace (reached by funicular) are spectacular. Popular, so reserve a table.

✉ Petřínské sady, Malá Strana ☎ 257 315 329

Novometsky Pivovar

One of a new generation of Czech brew-pubs, this restaurant serves a large menu of classic Czech dishes in large portions.

✉ Vodičkova 20, Nové Město ☎ 222 232 448; www.npivovar.cz

Pizzeria Rugantino

Authentic Italian trattoria just off Old Town Square serving salads, pies and pizzas cooked in a wood-fired oven.

✉ Dušní 4, Josefov ☎ 222 318 172; www.rugantino.cz

Rocky O'Reilly's

A friendly Irish restaurant and pub just off Wenceslas Square with a large menu of crowd-pleasing favourites.

✉ Štěpánská 32, Nové Město ☎ 222 231 060; www.rockyoreillys.cz

Take a picnic in the small park on Žofín Island (near the National Theatre), where there are panoramic views of Prague Castle.

Národní třída, Nové Město 9, 22, 23

U Kalicha

Immortalized by Jaroslav Hašek's novel, *The Good Soldier Švejk,* (the green-uniformed hero on the sign outside). U Kalicha serves traditional Czech fare and has a range of *Švejk* memorabilia.

✉ Na Bojišti 12, Vinohrady, Praha 2 ☎ 224 916 475; www.ukalicha.cz

Top activities

Bowling: Bowling Centrum RAN (Hotel Marriott).
✉ V celnici 10, Staré Město
☎ 221 033 020;
www.bowlingran.cz

Canoeing: on the Berounka River – experienced canoers and beginners (Saturdays and Sundays), Central European Adventures.
✉ Jáchymova 4, Josefov
☎ 222 328 879

Cycling: Central European Adventures and City Bike offer bike rental and bike tours.
Central European Adventures:
✉ Jáchymova 4, Josefov ☎ 222 328 879 (bicycle tours to Karlštejn and the Koněprusy Caves, also day trips around Prague). Closed Mondays. City Bike:
✉ Králodvorská 5, Staré Město
☎ 776 180 284; www.citybike-prague.com

Fitness centres: World Class Health Academy ✉ V celnici 10, Staré Město ☎ 221 033 033/ ✉ Václavské náměstí 22 ☎ 234 699 100. Fitness Club ✉ InterContinental Hotel, náměstí Curieových 43/5, Josefov ☎ 296 631 111

Golf: the nine-hole golf course at Golf Club Praha, behind Hotel Golf, has a putting green, driving range, pro-shop and restaurant (✉ Plzeňská, Motol, Praha 5 ☎ 257 216 584; www.gcp.cz). Erpet Golf Centrum offers an 18-hole virtual reality golf course, as well as astro-turf putting greens and driving platforms for some serious practice (✉ Strakonická 510, Smíchov, Praha 5 ☎ 257 321 177).

Jogging: there are plenty of open spaces for running in Prague including Stromovka Park, the Vyšehrad ramparts, around Strahov, Kampa Island and Letná. Avoid running along city streets to escape the car fumes.

Sports centres: the sports complex at the four-star Club Hotel Praha offers every athletic facility you can dream of from track and field to court games and gym and massage facilities.
✉ Pruhonice 400, Branik, Praha 4 ☎ 274 010 530

Swimming: there are indoor and outdoor pools at Podolí (✉ Podolská 74, Košíře, Praha 4 ☎ 241 433 952). There is also a beach at Džbán Reservoir with a special section for nude bathing (✉ Šárka Nature Reserve, Praha 6).

Tennis: this is a very popular sport in the Czech Republic and there are two dozen outdoor clay courts at Hamr Sports Complex.
✉ Zábehlická, Zábehlice, Praha 10 ☎ 272 772 762; www.hamrsport.cz

Best views

From the giant metronome on Letná Gardens – there used to be a statue of Stalin here (➤ 107)

Across Malá Strana from the Observatory on Petřín Hill (➤ 122)

Along the Vltava River valley from the ramparts of Vyšehrad (➤ 158)

Spectacular views of the city from the astronomical tower of the Klementínum (➤ 90–91)

Across Staré Město from the tower of Staroměstská radnice (Old Town Hall) (➤ 46–47)

From the Belvedere's garden terrace across to the castle walls and the bridges on the Vltava River (➤ 116–117)

Over the city once you have climbed the 287 steps up to the top of St Vitus's Cathedral tower (➤ 40–41)

From the Vltava River across Charles Bridge (➤ 89) to Staré Město from Kampa Island

Look down on the city at your feet from the south-facing terrace of the Starý kralovský palác (Old Royal Palace)

From the Prašná brána (Powder Gate) across the Obecní dům (Municipal House) and along Celetná towards the Old Town (➤ 156)

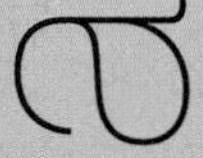

along the Royal Route

This walk follows the processional route taken by the kings and queens of Bohemia at their coronation.

Start at Obecní dům (➤ 155) and head down Celetná to Staroměstské náměstí.

The leading burghers and dignitaries of the town rode out to welcome their new monarch at the Powder Gate (➤ 156), before accompanying him past the cheering crowds on Celetná (➤ 85) to Old Town Square (➤ 96–97). Here the procession halted to hear professions of loyalty from the rector of the University and the mayor and council in the Old Town Hall (➤ 46–47).

Cross the square to Malé náměstí and on to Karlova. At the end of Karlova, cross Křižovnická to Křižovnícké náměstí (➤ 92–93) and the Charles Bridge (➤ 89).

Today Karlova is a quaint, twisting street, lined with galleries and souvenir shops, overshadowed by the fortress-like walls of the former Jesuit stronghold, the Klementinum (➤ 90–91). As the procession passed the Church of St Francis the King was greeted by the Order of the Knights of the Cross with the Red Star (➤ 92–93).

Cross the Vltava River to Mostecká and follow Malostranské náměstí round onto Nerudova (➤ 121). Climb the hill to the Castle.

At the Lesser Quarter Bridge Tower, the mayor handed over the keys to the city and the King then continued through Malostranské náměstí (➤ 119) to the tumultuous sound of bells from St Nicholas's Church (➤ 36–37). The processional route ends at the Matthias Gate, the ceremonial entrance to Prague Castle.

Distance 2.5km (1.5 miles)
Time 1.5 hours without stops
Start point Obecní dům ✉ Náměstí Republiky, Nové Město ✚ 10C
End point Pražský hrad ✉ Hradčany ✚ 4D
Lunch Square (££) ✉ Malostranské náměstí 5, Malá Strana
☎ 257 532 109

Best palaces

ARCIBISKUPSKÝ PALÁC (ARCHBISHOP'S PALACE)

This luxurious residence is hidden behind an impressive rococo façade. Unfortunately, the palace is closed to the public apart from special occcasions (➤ 111).

D3 Hradčanské náměstí 16, Hradčany Not open to the public 22, 23 to Pražský hrad

ČERNÍNSKÝ PALÁC (ČERNÍN PALACE)

Dominating the Hradčany upper quarter, Černín Palace is Prague's largest palace (➤ 110). The baroque building was constructed from 1669 to 1720.

C1 Loretánské náměstí, Hradčany Not open to the public 22, 23 to Pohořelec

DŮM PÁNŮ Z KUNŠTÁTU A PODĚBRAD (HOUSE OF THE LORDS OF KUNŠTÁT AND PODĚBRADY)

One of the city's oldest palace interiors accessible to the public (➤ 86). The vaulted cellars, the original ground floor, date back to the 13th century, and during the 15th century the palace was home to George of Poděbrady who was crowned King of Bohemia in 1458.

B8 Řetězová 3, Staré Město Summer: daily 11–6. Closed winter Inexpensive Staroměstská

LOBKOVICKÝ PALÁC (LOBKOWICZ PALACE)

Designed by architect Giovanni Battista Alliprandi, work began on this superb baroque building in 1703 and an additional floor was added in the 1760s. It was used for many purposes until 1971 when it became the West German Embassy and in 1989 was a place of refuge for many East Germans who walked through the fallen Berlin wall. A golden Trabant car can be seen in the palace gardens through the railings, in memory of that historic time.

C3 Vlašská 19, Malá Strana Not open to the public 12, 22, 23 to Malostranské náměstí

PRAŽSKÝ HRAD (PRAGUE CASTLE)

The towering Gothic spires of St Vitus's Cathedral beyond the neoclassical façade of Prague Castle can be seen from wherever you are in the city (► 44–45).

D4 Hradčany Castle complex: daily 5am–midnight. Premises: 26 Mar–Oct daily 9–5; Nov–15 Mar daily 9–4 22, 23 to Pražský hrad

SCHÖNBORNSKÝ PALÁC (SCHÖNBORN-COLLOREDO PALACE)

This mid-17th-century baroque palace fell into ruin in the 19th century but was repaired in 1917 and converted into apartments. In 1945, it became the American embassy as it is today.

C4 Tržiště 15, Malá Strana Not open to the public 12, 22, 23 to Malostranské náměstí

SCHWARZENBERSKÝ PALÁC (SCHWARZENBERG PALACE)

The Schwarzenberg Palace has an eye-catching, sgraffiti-adorned façade and impressive gables. It is now home to Prague's Military History Museum.

C3 Hradčanské náměstí 2, Hradčany 220 202 020 Check locally Inexpensive 22, 23 to Pražský hrad

ŠTERNBERSKÝ PALÁC (STERNBERG PALACE)

The Sternberg Palace houses the National Gallery's collection of European masters (► 48–49).

D3 Hradčanské náměstí 15, Hradčany Tue–Sun 10–6 22, 23 to Pražský hrad Malostranské

VALDŠTEJNSKÝ PALÁC (WALLENSTEIN PALACE)

This baroque palace (► 126–127), built for Albrecht of Wallenstein is the seat of the parliament of the Czech Republic (the Senate).

D5 Valdštejnské náměstí 4, Malá Strana 257 071 111 Sat–Sun 10–4 Inexpensive 12, 20, 22, 23

Best churches

BETLÉMSKÁ KAPLE (BETHLEHEM CHAPEL)

The twin gables of the Bethlehem Chapel (► 84–85) draw you to where Jan Hus preached in the 1400s. The chapel was reconstructed in the 1950s after being destroyed in the 18th century.

8B Betlémské náměstí, Staré Město Daily 10–5 Inexpensive

CHRÁM SVATÉHO MIKULÁŠ (ST NICHOLAS'S CHURCH)

See pages 36–37.

KATEDRÁLA SVATÉHO VÍTA (ST VITUS'S CATHEDRAL)

See pages 40–41.

KLÁŠTER SVATÉHO JIŘÍ (ST GEORGE'S CONVENT AND BASILICA)

See page 113.

KOSTEL PANNY MARIE PŘED TÝNEM (TÝN CHURCH)

The church's striking Gothic twin towers soar up from behind the gables of the former Týn School and can be seen for miles (► 91).

9C Týnská and Celetná, Staré Město May be open only for services due to reconstruction Cafés and restaurants nearby Staroměstská or Náměstí Republiky

KOSTEL PANNY MARIE VÍTĚZNÉ (CHURCH OF OUR LADY VICTORIOUS)

This 17th-century church became a focal point of the Counter-Reformation after Czech Protestantism was suppressed in 1621.

In 1628 a small wax effigy of the infant Jesus, 'Bambino di Praga', was given to the church and was thought to have miraculous powers (➤ 114).

5B Karmelitská 9, Malá Strana Mon–Sat 8.30–5.30, Sun 1–5

KOSTEL SVATÉHO JAKUBA (ST JAMES'S CHURCH)

Built on the site of an ancient Gothic church, the baroque St James's church has wonderful acoustics and many concerts and recitals are performed here (➤ 92).

10C Malá Štupartská, Staré Město Daily 9.30–12, 2–4

KOSTEL SVATÉHO MIKULÁŠ, STARÉ MĚSTO (ST NICHOLAS'S CHURCH, OLD TOWN)

St Nicholas's Church, in the Old Town (➤ 137), was once hemmed in on three sides by houses resulting in the twin towered façade having a southerly facing aspect rather than traditionally facing west.

9C Staroměstské náměstí, Staré Město Apr–Oct Mon noon–4, Tue–Sat 10–4, Sun noon–3; Nov–Mar Tue, Thu, Fri, Sun 10–noon, Wed 10–4

LORETÁNSKÁ KAPLE (LORETA SHRINE)

See pages 42–43.

Best places to take the children

ACTIVITIES

Paddle boats

Paddle boats are available for rent on Slovansky Island (also called Žofín Island).

✉ Malá Strana 🚇 Národní třída

Exhibition Grounds

The extensive Exhibition Grounds have an old-fashioned fun-fair, a swimming pool, the Seaworld aquarium and a planetarium that presents several shows daily between 2 and 5pm.

✉ Výstaviště, Holešovice, Praha 7 ☎ 220 103 111 🚋 5, 12, 14, 15, 17 to Výstaviště

Petřín Hill

Climb the hill with a picnic lunch and enjoy the wonderful views, or take the funicular to the top where there is a mini Gothic castle, botanic gardens, Mirror Maze and a mini Eiffel tower (► 122).

✉ Malá Strana 🚇 Národní třída, then tram 9, 22, 23 to Újezd

Detsky ostroff

A lovely, safe enclosed playground on a small island just off the Malá Strana side of the Vltava River.

✉ Entrance on Janáčkovo nábřeží (Jiráskův most), Malá Strana 🚇 Karlovo náměstí, then tram 4, 10, 16 to Zborovská

Tram rides

Prague's red-and-cream trams are fascinating to children; numbers 22 and 23 take the most scenic route.

MUSZEUMS

Muzeum hraček (Toy Museum)

The toy array at this castle museum spans 150 years and includes dolls, model houses, cars, aircraft, paddle steamers and much more.

✉ Jiřská 6, Hradčany ☎ 224 372 294 ⏲ Tue–Sun 🚌 22

Národní technické muzeum (National Technical Museum)

The Transport Hall has a wonderful collection of vintage cars, old trains, motorcycles and aeroplanes, as well as a simulated coal mine (➤ 120). There are also exhibits on photography and astronomy.

✉ Kostelní 42, Holešovice, Praha 7 ☎ 233 371 801 ⏲ Tue–Sun 9–5 Ⓜ Vltavská 🚌 1, 26

Zoologická zahrada (Prague Zoo)

Renovated since the floods of 2002, the zoo's tropical hall and giant komodo dragons must not be missed.

✉ U Trojského zámku 3, Troja, Praha 7 ☎ 220 399 111 ⏲ Daily 9–7 Ⓜ Nádraží Holešovice, then bus 112 to Zoologická zahrada

THEATRE

Don Giovanni Marionette Opera

Hand-crafted marionettes play the roles of the Mozart opera in this entertaining two-hour show.

✉ Kinsky Palace, Staré Město ☎ 224 216 365 ⏲ Daily at 6.30pm

Národní Divadlo Marionet (National Marionette Theatre)

It's well worth investigating the programme of productions here. The theatre has matinée and evening performances (➤ 146).

✉ Žatecká 1, Josefov ☎ 224 901 448 Ⓜ Staroměstská

Open spaces

Baroque gardens below Pražský hrad

There are fountains, arbours and balustrades dotted throughout these gardens; most impressive is the Wallenstein Palace garden.

5D Valdštejnské náměstí 3, Malá Strana Apr–Oct daily 10–6 Moderate Malostranská

Kampa Island

The 'Venice of Prague', Kampa Island is a lovely green area separated from Malá Strana by a tributary of the Vltava River known as the Devil's Channel.

6B At all times Free 12, 22, 23 to Hellichova or Malostranské náměstí or off the Charles Bridge down the stone stairs

Královská zahrada (Royal Gardens)
These beautiful 16th-century gardens are home to the Baroque Riding School, the sgraffitoed Ball-Game Hall and the elegant Belvedere (► 116–117).
4E Královská zahrada, Hradčany Apr–Oct daily 10–6 Free
22, 23 to Královský letohrádek or Pražský hrad

Petřín Hill
See page 122.

Valdštejnský palác a sady (Wallenstein Gardens)
See pages 126–127.

Vojanový sady (Vojan Gardens)
Hidden behind high walls these secluded gardens in the middle of Malá Strana were once part of the Archbishop's Palace and are still evocative of medieval times.
6D U Lužického semináře 17, Malá Strana Summer daily 8–7; winter daily 8–5 Free Malostranská

Vrtbovská zahrada (Vrtba Garden)
This 18th-century baroque garden is dotted with sculptures and has a fine staircase. There are wonderful views across Malá Strana from here.
4C Karmelitská 25, Malá Strana Apr–Oct daily 10–6
Inexpensive 12, 22, 23 to Malostranské náměstí

Zahrada na valech (Ramparts Garden)
This charming little park runs the breadth of the castle's south face and is filled with features, including an 18th-century fountain, an arboretum, an aviary and several pavilions.
4D Pražský hrad (Prague Castle), Hradčany Apr–Oct daily 10–6 Free Malostranská then uphill walk 22, 23 to Pražský hrad

Places to stay

Alchymist Grand Hotel and Spa (£££)
There are 20 suites and 26 rooms at this five-star hotel that range from simply luxurious to absolutely indulgent.
✉ Tržiště 19, Malá Strana ☎ 257 286 011; www.alchymisthotelresidence.com

Aria (£££)
This beautiful hotel has a musical theme with rooms named after musicians and floors labelled in different musical genre.
✉ Tržiště 9, Malá Strana ☎ 225 334 111; www.aria.cz

Bellagio (£££)
No expense was spared on the Italian design of the 46 rooms and suites in this sophisticated boutique hotel.
✉ U Milosrdných 2, Josefov ☎ 221 778 999; www.bellagiohotel.cz

Four Seasons Hotel Prague (£££)
The luxurious and elegant Four Seasons is in a fabulous riverside location near to Karlův most (Charles Bridge).
✉ Veleslavin 2a, Staré Město ☎ 221 427 000/221 427 777; www.fourseasons.com/prague

The Iron Gate (£££)
The Iron Gate offers 43 tastefully furnished suites and studios in a historic building which dates back to the 14th century.
✉ Michalská 19, Staré Město ☎ 225 777 777; www.irongate.cz

Josef (£££)
Designed by top architect Eva Jiřičná, the Josef is a sophisticated hotel popular with movie stars and others who appreciate elegant minimalism. There is an excellent gym and a pretty, private garden.
✉ Rybná 20, Staré Město ☎ 221 700 111/221 700 901; www.hoteljosef.com

Le Palais (£££)
The 4-star Le Palais is a belle époque architectural jewel of a hotel with 72 rooms and suites. Nineteenth-century refinement and modern luxury are perfectly combined here.
✉ U Zvonřaky 1, Vinohřady, Praha 2 ☎ 234 634 111; www.lepalais.cz

Radisson SAS Alcron (£££)
Thought to be one of Prague's most luxurious hotels, the Alcron has beautifully furnished rooms and sumptuous bathrooms. The 212-room hotel has kept its traditional feel yet has contemporary touches and is just off Václavské námestí.
✉ Štěpánská 40, Nové Město ☎ 222 820 000; www.prague.radissonsas.com

Romantik Hotel U Raka (£££)
Situated in the picturesque Nový Svět, this charming log-walled hotel is in great demand and has only six rooms, so book well in advance. The rooms are sumptuously furnished and the service is excellent. The terraced patio out back is sublime.
✉ Černínská 10, Hradčany ☎ 220 511 100; www.romantikhotel-uraka.cz

U Zlaté Studně (£££)
This hotel boasts some of the best views in Prague, starting with the baroque palace gardens just below. Peace and quiet are guaranteed here as the hotel is at the top of a closed, steep lane.
✉ U zlaté studně 166/4, Malá Strana ☎ 257 011 213; www.zlatastudna.cz

Speciality shops

Bat'a

One of the world's most famous shoe retailers, Bat'a returned to Prague after the Velvet Revolution and continues to produce footwear of the very highest quality.

✉ Václavské náměstí 6, Nové Mešto ☎ 224 218 133 🚇 Můstek

Big Ben

This is the perfect port of call if you've forgotten to pack your holiday reading matter. Only English-language books are on sale here, including information guides to Prague and many children's books.

✉ Malá Štupartská 5, Staré Město ☎ 224 826 565 🚇 Náměstí Republiky

Capriccio

This store boasts the largest selection of sheet music in Prague: more than 10,000 items in all, including jazz and classical scores – also CDs.

✉ Újezd 15, Malá Strana ☎ 257 320 165 🚌 12, 27, 57

Dům Sportu

Central shop with a comprehensive range of sportswear and sporting equipment.

✉ Jungmannova 28, Nové Město ☎ 224 212 347 🚇 Můstek

The Globe Bookstore and Coffeehouse (£)

This bookstore-cum-café is a good source for English-language versions of contemporary classics by writers such as Milan Kundera and Václav Havel.

www.bata.cz

✉ Pštrossova 6, Nové Mešto ☎ 224 934 203 Ⓜ Národní třída 🚌 6, 9, 17, 21, 22, 23, 51, 54, 58

Knihkupectví Na Můstku

Small, but useful bookshop selling a range of art glossies and books about Prague as well as general titles.

✉ Na přikopě 3, Nové Mešto ☎ 224 216 383 Ⓜ Můstek

Knihkupectví U Černé Matky Boží

Central bookshop with a good selection of maps and guidebooks in English and other languages.

✉ Celetná 34, Staré Mešto ☎ 224 211 155 Ⓜ Můstek

Kodak Express

Camera equipment including film and batteries and a 1-hour processing service.

✉ Branches at Ninohradská 6, Komunardů 19 and Metro Hradčanská

Philharmonia

The official representative of the Prague Philharmonia Orchestra stocks a comprehensive range of CDs, also DVDs, videos and books at competitive prices.

✉ Pařížská 13, Josefov ☎ 222 324 060 Ⓜ Staroměstská

Tobacco, Cigars & Pipes

An Aladdin's cave of Cuban cigars, tobacco and pipes.

✉ Pavilon, Vinohradská 50, Nové Mešto ☎ 224 233 125 🚌 11

U Jednorožce

One of Old Town Square's most distinguished historic houses, 'At the Unicorn' sells maps, guides, comics and a variety of postcards.

✉ Staroměstské náměstí 17, Staré Mešto ☎ 224 210 606 Ⓜ Staroměstská

Exploring

The view from the Charles Bridge at dusk: in the foreground, a procession of dramatic sculptures recedes into the distance; assembled behind them an extraordinary composition of gilded crosses, tented Gothic towers and baroque domes is silhouetted against the sunset. This is Prague in a nutshell. The city's extraordinary charms lie in the painstaking detail of its architecture – a gabled roof, an ornate railing, a sculpted house sign, a pair of Atlantes supporting a portal, a votive statue ensconced in a niche, a street lamp decorated with dancing maidens. Wherever you turn there is some magic to catch the eye.

This book focuses on Central Prague (Praha 1) which is divided into the following districts: Staré Město (Old Town), Nové Město (New Town), Malá Strana (Lesser Quarter), Josefov (Jewish Quarter) and Hradčany (Castle Quarter). Where reference has been made to anything in the outlying areas (Praha 2–10), the district name and Prague area number are given, eg Holešovice, Praha 7.

Staré Město Area

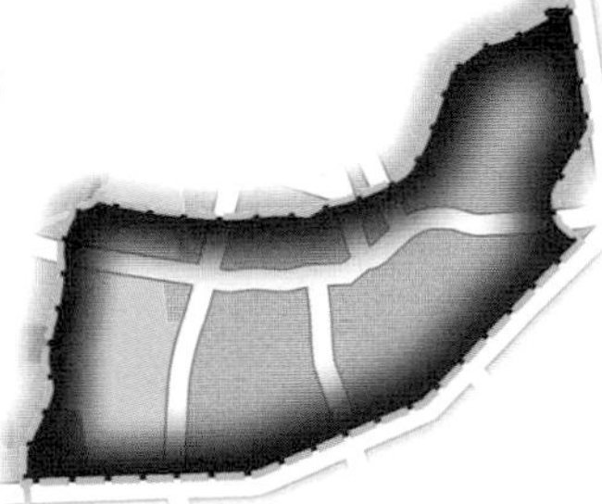

Beyond the Charles Bridge is Staré Město (Old Town), historically the most important of the areas that make up this great city. Staré Město is positioned on a bend in the Vltava River and grew up around Staroměstské náměstí (Old Town Square), still a popular meeting place and one of the prettiest squares in Europe, then stretching down to Karlův most (Charles Bridge) and east out to Celetná.

The southern section of Staré Město is a maze of narrow streets and arcaded courtyards that conceal gabled houses, brightly painted shop-fronts, churches and taverns. The streets are so narrow that trams have to make their way around the Old Town and not through it as kings once did en route to their coronations, when Staré Město was part of the 'Royal Route'. Contrasts abound here with steep Gothic spires and colourful baroque palaces standing alongside junk shops and internet cafés and fine restaurants next to more earthy pubs.

BETLÉMSKÁ KAPLE (BETHLEHEM CHAPEL)

The Bethlehem Chapel (➤ 70) was built by followers of the radical preacher Jan Milíč of Kroměříž between 1391 and 1394. In 1402 Jan Hus, was appointed rector and drew huge crowds to his sermons, which were given in Czech, rather than Latin. Hus was a charismatic figure, but his attacks on the wealth and corruption of the Catholic hierarchy did not endear him to his religious superiors.

He eventually overstepped the bounds of orthodoxy, arguing that the Pope had no authority over the Bohemian Church and that doctrine should be based on the scriptures alone. Hus was excommunicated in 1412 and the Bethlehem Chapel was closed. Summoned to defend his teachings at the Council of Constance two years later, Hus consented to leave the safe territory of Prague only after being issued with a guarantee of safe conduct by the Emperor Sigismund. But the Emperor went back on his word: Hus was arrested, condemned as a heretic and, on 6 July 1415, burned at the stake.

The decision to reconstruct the Chapel was taken in 1949. The prayer hall is trapezoid in form, the timber roof resting on plain stone supports. The total area measures 798sq m (8,590sq ft) – ample space for the congregations of 3,000 who came to hear Hus speak. Upstairs in the former preacher's house is an exhibition: 'The Bethlehem Chapel in Czech history and the tradition of non-Catholic thinking'.

8B Betlémské náměstí 4, Staré Město 224 248 595 Apr–Oct daily 10–6.30; Nov–Mar Tue–Sun 10–5.30. Closed 1 Jan, Easter Mon, 1 and 8 May, 5–6 July, 28 Oct, 24–26 Dec Moderate Cafés (£) near by Národní třída 6, 9, 18, 22

CELETNÁ

The street of bakers is one of the oldest in the city and was on the royal processional route. Its handsomely decorated baroque façades conceal in many cases Romanesque or Gothic foundations. An exception is the Cubist House of the Black Madonna (► 86). The house at No 36 is the former mint. Some of Prague's best known restaurants are on Celetná: House At the Golden Vulture (No 22), At the Spider (No 17) and At the Golden Stag (No 11). Celetná is also a good place to shop for glassware, jewellery and antiques.

9C Celetná, Staré Město Free Cafés (££), restaurants (£££) Náměstí Republiky

DŮM PÁNŮ Z KUNŠTÁTU A PODĚBRAD (HOUSE OF THE LORDS OF KUNSTAT AND PODEBRAD)

The medieval chambers of this former palace (► 68), with original Romanesque cross-vaulted ceilings and fireplaces, are now open to the public. Dating from about 1200, they once formed the ground floor of a building which was enlarged in the 15th century for the Lords of Kunstat and Podebrad. There is a small exhibition on its most famous resident, George of Podebrad, who became King of Bohemia in 1457.

8B Řetězová 3, Staré Město 224 212 299 May–Sep Tue–Sun 10–6 Národní třída Moderate 6, 9, 18, 22, 23

DŮM U ČERNÉ MATKY BOŽÍ (HOUSE OF THE BLACK MADONNA)

While Cubist painting is common in Europe, Cubist architecture is unique to Bohemia. Designed by Josef Gočár between 1911 and 1912, this innovative building was right at the cutting edge of the modernist movement, with its façades broken into multiple planes in order to create an unusual interplay of light and shade. Behind a grille on the first floor is the statue of the Madonna which gives the building its name. Upstairs is a beautiful café that looks just as it did when it opened in the 1920s.

Inside is a permanent exhibition on Czech Cubism from 1911 to 1919.

10C Ovocný trh 19, Staré Město 224 211 746 Tue–Sun 10–6. Closed 1 Jan, Easter Mon, 1 and 8 May, 5 and 6 July, 28 Oct, 24–6 Dec Moderate Náměstí Republiky 5, 8, 14

DŮM U KAMENNÉHO ZVONU (HOUSE AT THE STONE BELL)

This magnificent Gothic tower with its characteristic hipped roof was built as a palace for King John of Luxembourg around 1340. The sculpted decoration of the west façade was rediscovered in the 1960s, having long been concealed by a rococo face-lift. Make sure you don't overlook the stone bell on the corner of the building which gives the house its name. Concerts and exhibitions are held here and visitors can see original Gothic features, including extensive fragments of medieval wall painting. The ceiling beams, delicately painted with floral motifs, date from the reign of Charles IV.

9C Staroměstské náměstí 13, Staré Město 224 827 526
Tue–Sun 10–6. Closed 1 Jan, Easter Mon, 1 and 8 May, 5–6 Jul, 28 Oct, 24–6 Dec Inexpensive Staroměstská

KARLŮV MOST (CHARLES BRIDGE)

This remarkable sandstone bridge, designed in 1357 by Petr Parléř for King Charles IV, links the Old Town with the Lesser Quarter. In 1657 a bronze crucifix with a Hebrew inscription was erected on the bridge – the only ornament at that time. The idea caught on and now more than 30 sculptures adorn the parapets. Perhaps the finest of them, by Matthias Braun (1710), shows St Luitgard kissing Christ's wounds in a vision. The figure with the starry halo is St John of Nepomuk whose tortured body was hurled into the river from this spot in 1393 after he had dared to side with his archbishop against the king. The Old Town Bridge Tower, built in 1391, is also the work of Petr Parléř. The sculptures above the arch show St Vitus in the company of kings Wenceslas IV and Charles IV. Today, buskers (street musicians) and street traders bring the bridge to life.

6C Karlův most, Staré Město Malá Strana Tower: Apr–Oct daily 10–6. Staré Město Tower: Apr–May, Oct daily 10–7; Jun–Sep daily 10–10; Mar daily 10–6; Nov–Feb daily 10–5 Towers: inexpensive Staroměstská 12, 22

KAROLINUM

Founded in 1348 by Charles IV, the Karolinum is the oldest university in Central Europe. It acquired the house of the former mint master, Johlin Rothlev of Kutná Hora, in 1383 (until then classes had been held in churches or private houses). Although Rothlev's house was completely remodelled in the 18th century by František Kaňka, the exquisite oriel window protruding from the façade on Ovocný trh is a reminder of its medieval origins. The Karolinum's original premises are currently occupied by the university Rectorate.

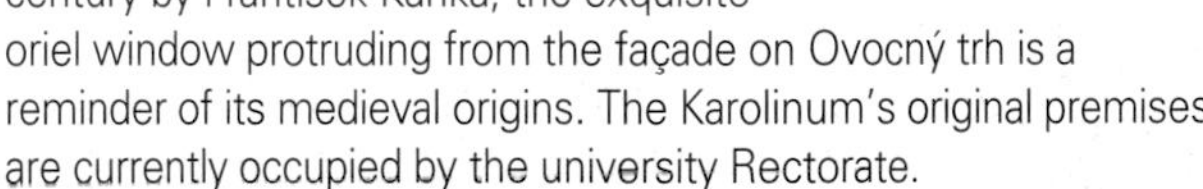

9C Železná 9, Staré Město 224 491 250; www.cuni.cz Můstek

KLEMENTINUM

When the Emperor Ferdinand I invited the Jesuits to Prague in 1556 to spearhead the Counter-Reformation, they moved into the former monastery of St Clement. In the 17th century the Karolinum (➤ 89) merged with the Klementinum and they undertook a building programme which lasted over 150 years.

The walls of the baroque fortress enclosed a college, schools, churches, a library, a theatre, an observatory and a printing shop. When the Jesuit Order was dissolved in 1773 the complex was taken over by the university; today it belongs to the National Library. The Chapel of Mirrors (1724–30) is also open for concerts.

8C Klementinum 190, Staré Město 221 663 111 May–Oct Mon–Fri 2–7, Sat–Sun 10–7; Mar–Apr, Nov–Dec Mon–Fri 2–6, Sat–Sun 11–7 Moderate Staroměstská 17, 18

KOSTEL PANNY MARIE PŘED TÝNEM (CHURCH OF OUR LADY BEFORE TÝN)

Most impressive at night when its gaunt, black steeples are eerily lit, Our Lady before Týn is the Old Town parish church (► 70). Although building started in 1380 under the supervision of Petr Parléř, work on the towers was not completed until 1511. For most of that period Týn Church was the stronghold of the Hussite Utraquists, who insisted on taking communion wine as well as bread (the symbolic gilded chalice which hung from the gable was melted down after the Counter-Reformation to make an effigy of the Virgin). The sculpted portal dates from 1390. The interior is a mix of Gothic and baroque styles. Over the high altar are paintings by Karel Škréta, dating from 1640 to 1660, while Gothic features include a pietà and a pewter font (1414). In front of the high altar is the tomb of the Danish astronomer, Tycho Brahe (1546–1601).

9C Staroměstské náměstí, Staré Město 222 322 801 Services Wed–Sat at 6pm, Sun 9.30am and 9pm Free Cafés (£), restaurants (£££) near by Staroměstská

KOSTEL SVATÉHO JAKUBA (ST JAMES'S CHURCH)

The Minorite Order of Franciscans commissioned this baroque church in 1689 after its 13th-century predecessor had been destroyed in a fire. The paintings in the nave, galleries and 21 side altars are by a variety of artists, including Franz Voget, Peter Brandl and Václav Reiner, who also contributed the effulgent *Martyrdom of St James* over the high altar. Equally remarkable is the stunning tomb of the Chancellor of Bohemia, Count Vratislav of Mitrovice, on the left-hand side of the nave. It was sculpted in marble and sandstone by Ferdinand Brokoff. A shrivelled arm which dangles just inside the door belonged to a jewel thief caught stealing here in the 16th century.

St James's (➤ 71) is renowned for its musical tradition. A choir sings at high Mass on Sundays, accompanied on the organ, a splendid baroque instrument dating from 1702. There are regular concerts and recitals here.

10C Malá Štupartská 6, Staré Město Mon–Sat 9.30–12.15, 2–4. Sun except for services 8, 9, 10.30, also for concerts Free Můstek

KŘIŽOVNICKÉ NÁMĚSTÍ (KNIGHTS OF THE CROSS SQUARE)

Dominating the eastern side of this square, which is named after the 13th-century guardians of the Judith Bridge and which is a popular place, is the façade of the Klementinum and the Jesuit Church of St Saviour (➤ 91). The knights' own Church of St Francis, a baroque building which dates from 1679 to 1688, is across the square.

The church's dome is thought to have been modelled on the dome of St Peter's in Rome.

An exhibition at the side of the church includes a visit to the medieval crypt, which is decorated with garishly painted baroque stalactites. The treasury contains a collection of jewelled monstrances, chalices, reliquaries and other religious objects which belonged to the Order, some dating back to the 16th century. Perhaps of greatest interest is a surviving span of the 12th-century Judith Bridge, complete with water stairs.

Standing in front of the church, near today's Charles Bridge, is an imposing statue of Charles IV, designed in 1848 by Jan Bendl.

7B Křižovnické náměstí, Staré Město Exhibition: Apr–Oct Tue–Sun 10–6; Nov–Mar Tue–Sun 10–5 Inexpensive Staroměstská 17, 18

MUZEUM BEDŘICHA SMETANY (SMETANA MUSEUM)

The life and work of the 'father of Czech Music', Bedřich Smetana (1824–84), are traced here through letters, documents, scores and musical instruments. Smetana studied piano and composition in Prague, where he heard Liszt and, later, Berlioz perform. A fervent patriot, whose music helped inspire the Czech national revival of the 19th century, he is best known abroad for his emotionally charged symphonic

poem, *Ma vlast* (My homeland) – the famous second movement evokes the swirling currents of the Vltava. He also composed some fine chamber music, as well as numerous operas for the National Theatre, including *The Bartered Bride* and *The Kiss*. Smetana's later life was clouded by personal tragedy: in 1874 he went profoundly deaf after suffering from tinnitus and later lost his reason, dying in an asylum.

7B Novotného lávka 1, Staré Město 222 222 082 Wed–Mon 10–12, 12.30–5 Moderate Staroměstská 17, 18 to Lávka

STAROMĚSTSKÁ RADNICE

See pages 46–47.

STAROMĚSTSKÉ NÁMĚSTÍ (OLD TOWN SQUARE)

As early as the 12th century the Old Town Square was a thriving market place. Merchants from all over Europe conducted their business here and in the Ungelt (➤ 98), a courtyard behind the Týn Church. The square was also a place of execution: among the victims were the Hussite rebel Jan Želivský and the 27 Protestant noblemen who died here following the Battle of the White Mountain in 1620 (they are commemorated by white crosses set in the pavement in front of Old Town Hall). Jan Hus, the father of Czech Protestantism, died in Constance, but his monument, a stark sculpture by Ladislav Šaloun (1915), stands in the centre of the square.

Today the Old Town Square is full of outdoor cafés, and at Easter and Christmas, it is transformed into a marketplace, with wooden huts selling all kinds of small crafts and Czech delicacies. Crowds mill around under the Astronomical Clock on the Old Town Hall (➤ 46–47) as it performs its mesmerizing hourly routine. But the square's chief glory is its architecture: the Renaissance and baroque façades of the houses conceal Gothic substructures and Romanesque cellars. The beautiful rococo embellishments on the Golz-Kinsky Palace, dating from 1765 (No 12 east side) are by Kilián Dientzenhofer. Franz Kafka went to school here in the 1890s. Directly in front of the Týn Church, the ribbed vaulting in the 14th-century Týn School arcade has survived.
9C Staroměstské náměstí, Staré Město Cafés (££), restaurants (£££) Free Staroměstská

STAVOVSKÉ DIVADLO (ESTATES THEATRE)

This famous theatre was built between 1781 and 1783 for Count F A Nostitz-Rieneck, who wanted to raise the cultural profile of the city. On 29 October 1787, the count had his wish when Mozart's opera *Don Giovanni* received its world première here after being rejected by the more conservative Viennese theatre managers. 'The people of Prague understand me', the composer is reported to have said after conducting the performance from the piano. In 1984 Miloš Forman shot the relevant scenes of his Oscar-winning film *Amadeus* in the auditorium, drawing attention to the need for renovation. That work was completed in the 1990s.

www.narodnidivadlo.cz
9B Ovocný trh 1, Staré Město 224 902 231 For concerts and tours Free Café (££) Můstek

UNGELT

From the 12th to the 18th centuries, this courtyard behind the Týn Church was a centre of commerce, where merchants paid *ungelt*, or customs duties. There was also a hostel offering accommodation for travellers here. The complex of 18 buildings dates from the 16th century onwards and has been restored as shops, hotels and offices. The Granov Palace (Granovský palác), built on the northern side of the square for a wealthy tax collector in 1560, is one of the most distinguished Renaissance buildings in Prague, with sgraffito depicting biblical and classical themes and a magnificent loggia.

✚ 9C ✉ Týnský dvůr, Staré Město ⑪ Restaurant in Hotel Ungelt (£££); others (££) Ⓜ Staroměstská

HOTELS

Betlem Club (££)

The name is a give away – this small hotel is situated just across the street from the Bethlehem Chapel, where the reformer Jan Hus preached in the 15th century. The hotel allows easy access to the Old Town and the bars and restaurants on the square.

Betlémské náměstí 9, Staré Město 222 221 575; www.betlemclub.cz Národní třída 6, 9, 22, 23

Černy slon (£££)

A tastefully reconstructed, UNESCO-protected 14th-century house, only a stone's throw from Old Town Square. Rooms are spacious and furnished with antiques. No lift (elevator).

Týnská 629/1, Staré Město 222 321 521; www.hotelcernyslon.cz Náměstí Republiky

Hotel Paříž (£££)

An eye-catching neo-Gothic building with art nouveau flourishes, the Paříž has undergone extensive restoration work and is now considered to be one of the city's top hotels.

U Obecního domu 1, Staré Město 222 195 195 Náměstí Republiky 5, 8, 14

Pension Unitas (£)

Popular with everyone from backpackers to senior citizens, this spotless 36-room pension is in a great location close to the heart of the city. Non-smoking throughout.

Bartolomějská 9, Staré Město 224 217 555; www.unitas.cz Národní třída 6, 9, 22, 23

RESTAURANTS

Bellevue (£££)

The aptly named Bellevue boasts stunning views of the castle and river. World-class cuisine within a formal, elegant setting. There is a lovely summer terrace and jazz accompanies Sunday lunch.

Smetanovo nábřeží 18, Staré Město 222 221 443 Národní třída 17, 18 to Karlovy lázné; 6, 9 to Národní divaldo

Café Louvre (£)
Franz Kafka used to discuss philosophy here in the early 1900s. The upstairs restaurant is a friendly, no-frills eating house that keeps pool tables in the back room. Serves breakfast.
✉ Národní 20, Staré Město ☎ 224 930 949; www.cafelouvre.cz Ⓜ Národní třída 🚋 6, 9, 18, 22, 23

Dahab (££)
A *souk*-like interior adds to the whole experience at this reasonably priced Middle Eastern restaurant. Excellent *baklava*. There are a variety of teas and hookah pipes on the menu, and belly dancers perform most weekend nights.
✉ Dlouhá 3, Staré Město ☎ 224 827 375; www.dahab.cz Ⓜ Náměstí Republiky 🚋 8, 14 to Dlouhá třída

Don Giovanni (££)
A welcoming trattoria, only a stone's throw from the Vltava. The *scaloppina di vitello* is recommended. The owner is proud of his selection of more than 30 varieties of home-made grappa.
✉ Karoliny světlé 34, Staré Město ☎ 222 222 060; www.dongiovanni.cz Ⓜ Národní třída 🚋 17, 18, 51, 54

Káva, Káva, Káva (£)
This busy café has the best coffee and espresso in town. It also serves pastries, *panini* and wine and has internet facilities. The entire café is a WiFi hotspot.
✉ Národní 37, Staré Město ☎ 224 228 862 Ⓜ Národní třída

Kogo (££)
A buzzing, trendy Italian restaurant with an empahisis on fresh ingredients, serving up delicious favourites.
✉ Havelska 27, Staré Město ☎ 224 214 543; www.kogo.cz. Also at ✉ Slovanský dům, Na příkopě 22, Nové Město ☎ 221 451 259

Klub architectů (£)
See pages 60–61.

La Bodeguita Del Mario (££)
Latin music, pitchers of *mojitos* and Cuban cooking draw the crowds at this busy, stylish restaurant and bar.
✉ Karlova 20, Staré Město ☎ 222 221 218 Ⓜ Staroměstská 🚋 17, 18, 51

La Provence (£££)
From the red leather booths to the silvered mirror over the oak bar, this is the closest you'll get to a real French bistro experience in Prague.
✉ Štupartská 9, Staré Město ☎ 257 535 050; www.kampagroup.cz
Ⓜ Náměstí Republiky 🚋 5, 14

Lotos (£)
One for the vegetarians, serving organic, vegan and marcobiotic food. Non-smoking throughout. A health-food store is attached.
✉ Platnéřská 13, Staré Město ☎ 222 322 390 Ⓜ Staroměstská

Mama Lucy (£)
A stylish interior with a casual atmosphere. Mama Lucy serves up Mexican fare just off the Old Town Square.
✉ Dlouhá 2, Staré Město ☎ 222 327 207

Reykjavik (££)
Centrally located between the Old Town Square and Charles Bridge, this Icelandic establishment serves Scandanavian and international cuisine and is renowned for its seafood dishes.
✉ Karlova 20, Staré Město ☎ 222 221 218; www.reykjavik.cz
Ⓜ Staroměstská

Rybí trh (£££)
'The Fish Market' is located in the Ungelt courtyard behind the Týn Church. The freshwater fish, sea fish and shellfish are expensive but worth it, and the wine list is excellent.
✉ Týn 5, Staré Město ☎ 224 895 447 Ⓜ Staroměstská

SHOPPING

ART AND ANTIQUES

Art Deco Galerie

Delve into this delightful old store which has an eclectic mix of household items, decorations, clothes and accessories from the 1920s through to the 1960s.

✉ Michalská 21, Staré Město ☎ 224 223 076

Galerie Art Praha

A representative selection of some of the finest contemporary works by Czech artists, including distinguished names like Bohumír Dvorsky and Karel Souček.

✉ Staroměstské náměstí 20, Staré Město ☎ 224 211 087 Ⓜ Staroměstská

Galerie České Plastiky

A gallery that focuses exclusively on post-1900 Czech sculpture, including statues and busts by the great Otto Gutfreund, Jan Hána and Emanuel Kodet.

✉ Revoluční 20, Nové Město ☎ 222 310 684 Ⓜ Náměstí Republiky

Galerie Jakubská

Permanent exhibition of work by modern Czech artists, and temporary exhibitions by artists from Russia and elsewhere.

✉ Jakubská 4, Staré Město ☎ 224 827 926; www.galeriejakubska
Ⓜ Náměstí Republiky

Galerie Pallas

Located in the old Ungelt courtyard, this gallery concentrates on Cubist, Expressionist and Surrealist works by such 20th-century masters as Jan Čapek, Emil Filla and Antonín Procházko.

✉ Týn 1, Staré Město ☎ 224 895 411 Ⓜ Staromestská

Galerie Peithner-Lichtenfels

A small, well-established gallery dealing in works by 19th- and 20th-century Czech masters, including Otto Gutfreund, Bohumil Kubišta and Toyen (Marie Čermínová).

✉ Michalská 12, Staré Město ☎ 224 227 680 Ⓜ Můstek

DEPARTMENT STORES AND SHOPPING MALLS

Černa Růže

This boutique-filled shopping arcade in the city centre showcases such designer names as Karl Lagerfeld, Pierre Cardin and Elazar Leatherware.

✉ Na příkopě 12, Nové Město ☎ 221 014 111; www.cernaruze.cz
Ⓜ Můstek

Tesco

You'll find everything you need over the four floors here: there's a large grocery section, as well as clothing, shoes and houseware.

✉ Národní 26, Nové Město ☎ 222 003 111; www.tesco-shop.cz
Ⓜ Národní třída 🚋 6, 9, 12, 22, 23

SOUVENIRS

Blue Praha

A trendy Czech souvenir store selling glasswear, artistic T-shirts, hats, fine postcards and other classy mementoes of Prague.

✉ Malé náměstí 14, Staré Město ☎ 224 216 717 Ⓜ Staroměstská

Botanicus & Apothicus

Everything on sale here has come from an organic farm 30km (18 miles) outside Prague. Spices, herbal remedies and candles etc.

✉ Týnský dvůr 3, Staré Město ☎ 224 895 446 🕒 Daily 10am–6.30pm
Ⓜ Náměstí Republiky

Celetná Crystal

A large store selling a wide range of garnets, amber, porcelain and Bohemain crystal.

✉ Celetná 17, Staré Město ☎ 222 324 022 Ⓜ Náměstí Republiky

Crystallino

A huge emporium of Czech crystal and glass, in any form you can dream of, from chandeliers to Champagne glasses.

✉ Celetná 12, Staré Město ☎ 224 225 173; www.crystallino.cz
Ⓜ Staromeštská 🚋 17, 18

Havelské tržiště

This central fruit and vegetable market also features many souvenir and craft stalls.

✉ Havelská, Staré Město 🚇 Můstek

Manufaktura

A gift shop with an emphasis on products made from natural materials. A wide range of traditional wooden toys, Christmas ornaments, glassware and handmade soap and cosmetics.

✉ Melantrichova 17, Staré Město ☎ 221 632 481 🚇 Můstek

Moser

A selection of superb quality porcelain and crystal if money is no object. Crystal and porcelain made in Karlovy Vary (or Carlsbad) and also porcelain from Meissen and Herend.

✉ Na příkopě 12, Nové Město ☎ 224 211 293; www.moser-glass.com 🚇 Můstek

Old Town Square Market

Around the edge of the square, kiosks sell crafts and souvenirs, including scarves, ceramics, wooden toys and wrought-iron work.

✉ Staroměstské náměstí, Staré Město ☎ None 🚇 Staroměstská

Porcela Plus

Czech crystal direct from Svá and Sázavou in the Moravian highlands. Stocks a variety of designs, including frosted vases, coloured wine glasses and crystal beer mugs.

✉ Na příkopě 17, Staré Město ☎ 224 239 653 🚇 Můstek

SPECIALITY SHOPS

Big Ben Bookshop

This English bookstore is the perfect port of call if you've forgotten to pack your holiday reading. A good range of novels by Czech authors and guides to Prague.

✉ Malá Štupartská 5, Staré Město ☎ 224 826 565; www.bigbenbookshop.com 🚇 Náměstí Republiky

Knihkupectví U Černé Matky Boži
A smallish central bookshop with a good selection of English-language fiction, maps and guidebooks.
✉ Celetná 34 Staré Město ☎ 242 222 349 Ⓜ Náměstí Republiky

ENTERTAINMENT

BARS

Bombay Cocktail Bar
This lively cocktail bar above Rasoi Indian restaurant is great place for a few gin and tonics after sampling the north Indian cusine on offer in the cellar downstairs.
✉ Dlouhá 13, Staré Město ☎ 222 328 400; www.rosoi.cz
🚋 Trams 5, 8, 14 to Dlouhá třída

Chapeau Rouge
Open until 5am, this bar is often crowded and always lively. The music gets louder as the hours grow smaller.
✉ Jakubská 2, Staré Město ☎ 222 316 328 Ⓜ Staroměstská

James Joyce
Cosy Irish pub with English, Irish and Czech beer, stouts and ales.
✉ Liliová 10, Staré Město ☎ 224 248 793

Roxy
This popular club attracts a loyal clientele that appreciates its run-down look and relaxed atmosphere.
✉ Dlouhá 33, Staré Město ☎ 224 826 296; www.roxy.cz Ⓜ Náměstí Republiky 🚋 Trams 8, 14 to Dlouhá třída

U Vejvodu
A classic Czech beer hall with efficient waiters and excellent food.
✉ Jilská 4, Nové Město ☎ 224 219 999; www.uvejvodu.cz
Ⓜ Národní třída

DISCOS AND CLUBS

La Fabrique

A fun disco with tables, a couple of dance floors and a varied crowd of all ages.

✉ Uhelný trh 2, Staré Město ☎ 224 233 137; www.lafabrique.cz
Ⓜ Národní třída

Reduta Jazz Club

One of the oldest jazz clubs in Prague, this is where American President Bill Clinton jammed with his saxaphone in 1994.

✉ Národní 20, Staré Město ☎ 224 933 487; www.redutajazzclub.cz
Ⓜ Národní třída

Ungelt Jazz & Blues Club

A small club in the 15th-century cellar of a Renaissance building behind Týn Church. A mix of blues, funk and jazz supplied by top Czech performers, with shows every night from 8pm.

✉ Týn 2, Staré Město ☎ 224 895 748; www.jazzblues.cz
Ⓜ Náměstí Republiky

U Staré Paní

'At the Old Lady' is a sophisticated cellar jazz club that attracts serious names from all over Europe and North America.

✉ Michalská 9, Staré Město ☎ 224 228 090; www.ustarepani.cz 🕐 Daily 7pm–2am Ⓜ Staroměstská

THEATRES AND CONCERT HALLS

Theatre Animato

✉ Na příkopě 10, Nové Město ☎ 222 244 358 Ⓜ Můstek

Ta Fantastika

✉ Karlova 8, Staré Město ☎ 222 221 366; www.tafantastika.cz
Ⓜ Staroměstská

Hradčany, Malá Strana and Beyond

Hradčany, on the left bank of Vltava River, is dominated by 16th-century Prague Castle, primarily a tourist attraction with its cathedral, museums and galleries, but also a seat of government – the President and his ministers have their offices here. Nowadays, many of the mansions and palaces are used as government offices, museums or even restaurants, and monuments in the surrounding neighbourhoods bear witness to the influence of Mozart and Joseph Stalin.

Malá Strana (Lesser Quarter), beneath the castle, is distinguished by the green of its gardens and orchards, created in the 17th century by the aristocrats who built their palaces here. The film *Amadeus*, which chronicles the life of Mozart, was filmed here, using the 18th-century architecture to create an illusion of Vienna at that time. Crowning Malostranské náměstí is the majestic, green-domed Church of St Nicholas. Nearer the Vltava, the small neighbourhood of Na Kampě is perfect for an evening stroll.

The area of Smíchov lies to the south, its highlights being the Mozart Museum and concerts that take place at Villa Bertramka.

The districts of Letná, Bubeneč and Holešovice spread out to the north and east where you'll find an art museum, a giant Metronome and a few relics from Prague's Communist past.

BERTRAMKA (MOZART MUSEUM)

This hillside villa, the home of the soprano Josefina Dušek and her composer husband František, was where Wolfgang Amadeus Mozart stayed on his visits to Prague in 1787 and 1791. Although the house was badly damaged by fire in 1873, the rooms Mozart occupied have survived and now contain a small exhibition on the composer and his happy relationship with the Bohemian capital. The most highly valued items, apart from the manuscripts, are his harpsichord and a lock of his hair. But his presence can best be felt in the lovely garden. It was here, on the night of 28 October 1787, that Mozart dashed off the sublime overture to his opera, *Don Giovanni*, just one night before the première was given in the Estates Theatre (► 97).

www.bertramka.cz

13J Mozartova 169, Smíchov, Praha 5 257 316 753 Apr–Oct daily 9–6; Nov–Mar daily 9.30–4 Inexpensive Café (£) Anděl then tram 9 to Bertramka Concerts Wed and Sat 5pm (held outside in summer)

BÍLÁ HORA (WHITE MOUNTAIN)

In the space of an hour, on 8 November 1620, the Catholic Habsburg army routed the Czech Protestants on this hillock

outside Prague, deciding the fate of Bohemia for the next 300 years. The battle is commemorated by a small stone monument and the Church of Our Lady of Victories (1704–14).

Also in the park is the Renaissance hunting lodge Letohrádek hvězda (Star Castle), built between 1555 and 1557 by Ferdinand of Tyrol. The castle now contains exhibitions devoted to the work of the writer Alois Jirásek and the painter Mikoláš Aleš.

www.hrady.cz

1E (off map) Obora Hvezda 160 00, Liboc, Praha 6 Castle: 235 357 938 Castle: May–Sep Tue–Sun 10–6; Apr, Oct Tue–Sun 10–5 Castle: inexpensive 8, 22 to Vypich, or bus 179 from Petřín

BŘEVNOVSKÝ KLÁŠTER (BŘEVNOV MONASTERY)

There has been a monastery in Břevnov since AD993, although the present baroque complex, designed by Christoph and Karl Dientzenhofer, dates from 1708 to 1745. The monastery has now been returned to the Benedictines. The remarkable St Margaret's Church, built over a Romanesque crypt, has stunning oval ceiling frescoes by Johann Steinfels, depicting scenes from the legend of St Adalbert, while the Theresian Hall has a magnificent painting of Blessed Günther by Kosmas Assam.

www.brevnov.cz

1E (off map) Markétská 28, Břevnov, Praha 6 220 406 111 Apr–Oct Sat–Sun 10, 2, 4; Nov–Mar Sat–Sun 10, 2 or by appointment Moderate 22, 25

ČERNÍNSKÝ PALÁC (ČERNÍN PALACE)

So much stone was used in the construction of this vast palace (➤ 68), with a façade stretching the entire length of Loretánské náměstí (135m/443ft), that it was said that the builders were being paid by the cubic metre. Certainly the palace's original owner, Count Jan Černín of Chudenice, Imperial Ambassador to Venice, spared no expense on the interior decoration – the work of the sculptor, Matthias Braun and the painter Václav Reiner, among others. In 1948, 20 years after the palace was acquired by the Ministry of Foreign Affairs, Jan Masaryk, son of the founder of Czechoslovakia and the only non-Communist member of the government, fell to his death from an upper floor window into the courtyard below. It is now widely believed that Masaryk was murdered on the orders of Stalin.

✚ 1C ✉ Loretánské náměstí 5, Hradčany ☎ None 🕘 Not open to public 🚌 22, 23

CHRÁM SVATÉHO MIKULÁŠ

See pages 36–37.

HRADČANSKÉ NÁMĚSTÍ (HRADČANY SQUARE)

This is a square of stunning Renaissance and baroque façades. The Archbishop's Palace (No 16) was given its eye-catching rococo face-lift in 1764 by the architect Johan Wirch, and is adorned with the family crest of Archbishop Antonín Příchovský (➤ 68). Across the square is the Renaissance Schwarzenberg Palace, which features what is considered the best sgraffito in Prague. The yellow-fronted Tuscany Palace (No 5), once owned by the Duke of Tuscany, dates from 1689 to 1691. Jaroslav Bořita of Martinitz gave his name to the handsome palace at No 8.

3D Hradčanské náměstí, Hradčany Café (£) 22

KATEDRÁLA SVATÉHO VÍTA

See pages 40–41.

KLÁŠTER SVATÉHO JIŘÍ (ST GEORGE'S CONVENT AND BASILICA)

St George's Convent houses the National Gallery's collection of Czech Mannerist and baroque art, and adjoining it is the Basilica, one of the oldest religious foundations in Prague, dating back to 920 and reconstructed in its present Romanesque form after a fire in 1142 (the baroque façade is a 17th-century addition). To the right of the entrance to the crypt is the painted wooden tomb of the founder, Prince Vratislav.

The exhibition in the convent begins with a display of Mannerist works by artists from the court of the Emperor Rudolph II: Bartholomeus Spranger, Hans von Aschen, Benedikt Wurzelbauer and Adrian de Vries – don't miss his superb sculpture *Stepping Horse* (*c*1610). The National Gallery's outstanding collection of baroque paintings and sculptures can be found on the first floor. Many of the Bohemian and Silesian artists exhibited here played a key role in beautifying Prague's churches and monasteries in the 17th and 18th centuries. They include Škreta, impressively represented by altarpieces, portraits and easel paintings, Peter Brandl, Václav Reiner and the sculptor Matthias Braun. Look out for some outstanding portraits by Jan Kupecký, notably *Self-Portrait with Wife* (after 1725) and Ignaz Platzer, a master of the rococo whose commissions included the decoration of the Church of St Nicholas in the Lesser Quarter.

4D Jiršké námsětí 33, Hradčany 224 373 368; 224 372 434 Tue–Sun 9–5 Moderate Café (£), restaurants (££–£££) near by 22, 23 to Pražský hrad

KOSTEL PANNY MARIE VÍTĚZNÉ (OUR LADY VICTORIOUS)

The chief attraction of this 17th-century church (➤ 70–71) is a wax effigy of the infant Jesus, known by its Italian name 'Il Bambino di Praga'. Believed to have miracle-working properties, the statue was brought from Spain in 1628 by Polxena of Lobkowicz and presented to the Carmelite nuns.

www.pragjesu.info

5B Karmelitská 9, Malá Strana 257 533 646 Museum: Mon–Sat 9.30–5.30, Sun 1–6. Church: Mon–Sat 8.30–7, Sun 8.30–8 Free 12, 22, 23

KOSTEL SVATÉHO TOMÁŠE (ST THOMAS'S CHURCH)

This church was established for the Order of the Augustinian hermits by King Wenceslas II, 1285, at the same time as the neighbouring Augustinian monastery, and has undergone many reincarnations over the centuries, the latest between 1723 and 1731 after it was damaged by lightning. The ceiling is covered in frescoes by Václav Reiner depicting the life of St Augustine and, in the dome, the legend of St Thomas. Amazingly, Reiner completed the work in just two years. Other distinguished artists, including Karel Škréta and the sculptor Ferdinand Brokoff, also contributed to the décor, while the paintings (copies) over the high altar, of St Thomas and St Augustine, were commissioned from Rubens (the originals are now in the Šternberský palác ➤ 48–49).

5C Josefská 8, Malá Strana 257 532 675 Daily. Mass in English Sun 11am Free Malostranská 12, 22, 23

KRÁLOVSKÁ ZAHRADA (ROYAL GARDENS)

These delightful gardens with wonderful views were laid out in 1534 in the style of the Italian Renaissance. Four years later, work began on the Belvedere, the handsome summer house presented by Ferdinand I to his wife, Anna Jagiello. A magnificent arcaded building with a copper roof resembling an upturned ship's hull, it was completed in 1564 by Paolo Della Stella, who also designed the mythological reliefs. The palace is now used for exhibitions. The sgraffitoed Ball Game Hall at the eastern end of the gardens is the work of the Czech architect, Bonifaz Wohlmut, and was given its name by courtiers who played a form of tennis here. Tulips grow in the gardens every spring – another reminder

of Ferdinand I, who introduced the flower to Europe from Turkey in the 16th century. Near the entrance is the Lion's Court, once a menagerie exhibiting bears, panthers, tigers and other wild beasts.

4E Královsky letohrádek, Hradčany Castle information: 224 373 368 Gardens: Apr–Oct daily 10–6; gardens on the bastion and gardens on the terrace open all year Free Restaurant (£££) 22, 23

LAPIDÁRIUM

Located in an art nouveau pavilion in Výstaviště (the Exhibition Ground), this is a fascinating review of Czech sculpture from the 11th to the 19th centuries, with explanatory leaflets in English and other languages. One of the earliest exhibits is a beautifully ornamented column from the crypt of the 11th-century Basilica of St Vitus; other displays include the Krocín fountain, a remarkable Renaissance monument which used to stand on Old Town Square, and the 9m-high (30ft) Bear Gate, also known as the Slavata Portal, which once adorned a beautiful baroque garden in the Smíchov district. Ferdinand Brokoff's statues of St Ignatius and St Francis Xavier, now adorning the Charles Bridge, are copies. The originals exhibited here were torn down in the floods of 1890.

28R Výstaviště 422, Holešovice, Praha 7 233 375 636 Tue–Fri 12–6, Sat–Sun 10–6 Inexpensive Cafés (£) Vltavská then tram 5 or 12 to Výstaviště 5, 12, 17

LENNONOVA ZED' (LENNON WALL)

Opposite the French embassy on Velkopřevoske náměstí, Kampa Island in Malá Strana, this stretch of wall was painted with democratic and pacifist graffiti following John Lennon's death in 1980. A game of cat-and-mouse ensued between police and artists as the wall was continually whitewashed and repainted. After the Velvet Revolution it was allowed to remain, at the request of the French ambassador.

5B Velkopřevoské náměstí, Malá Strana 12, 27, 57

LORETA

See pages 42–43.

MALOSTRANSKÉ NÁMĚSTÍ (LESSER TOWN SQUARE)

The former market square of Malá Strana dates from 1257. Looming over the charming ensemble of baroque buildings is St Nicholas's Church and former Jesuit College (➤ 36–37). Many of the arcaded houses have now been converted into cafés and restaurants.

The centrepiece of the square is the attractive Renaissance Town Hall (1617–22) on the eastern side. Next door is the house At the Flavins, with a colourful fresco of the Annunciation.

5C Malostranské náměstí, Malá Strana Cafés (£), restaurants (££–£££) Malostranská 12, 22

MALTÉZSKÉ NÁMĚSTÍ (MALTESE SQUARE)

This neighbourhood has been associated with the Order of the Knights of Malta since 1169. At the corner of Lázeňská is the former convent of the Order – Maltese crosses can still be seen on the main door and under the roof. Two impressive Gothic towers stand guard over the entrance to the Church of Our Lady Below the Chain, where a painting by Karel Škréta, decorating the main altar, depicts the victory of the Maltese Knights over the Turks at Lepanto in 1571. At the southern end of the square are two grand palaces: the brilliant pink-and-white Palais Turba, now the Japanese Embassy, and the ornate Nostitz Palace (open for chamber music concerts), which belongs to the Dutch Embassy.

5B Maltézské náměstí, Malá Strana Restaurants (£££) 12, 22, 23 to Malostranské náměstí

NÁRODNÍ TECHNICKÉ MUZEUM (NATIONAL TECHNICAL MUSEUM)

The vast, glass-roofed central hall is the main attraction of this museum, with its exhibition on the history of transport, featuring a fascinating array of more than 500 types of vehicles, machines and models. Suspended from the ceiling is the skeleton of an early powered glider dating from 1905 and J Kašpar's Bleriot-XI monoplane of 1910. A magnificent steam engine and tender, built in Prague for the Austrian State Railways in 1911, dwarfs everything else in the locomotives exhibition, and a wonderful collection of early automobiles starts with an 1893 Benz 'Viktoria'. Later automobile models on show include some 1970s and '80s Skoda coupés. The Czechs' own Skoda Works are represented by a wood-upholstered fire engine from 1928. Among the 40,000 items displayed elsewhere in the museum are a variety of film cameras, clocks, astrolabes, sextants, phonographs and much else besides. Visits to the simulated mining gallery are by guided tour only.

www.ntm.cz

26N · Kostelní 42, Holešovice, Praha 7 · 220 399 111 · Tue–Fri 9–5, Sat–Sun 10–6 · Inexpensive · Vltavská, Hradčanksá · 1, 8, 25, 26 to Letenské náměstí

NERUDOVA

This street honours Pavel Neruda (1834–91), whose short stories capture perfectly the small-town atmosphere of 19th-century Prague, and who was born at No 47. It's a steep climb to the top – Nerudova was originally called Spur Street after the brake which was applied to coaches on their descent. On your way you will see some wonderful 18th-century house signs (numbers were not introduced until the 1770s). Look out for The Red Eagle (No 6), The Three Fiddles (No 12), The Golden Cup (No 16), The Golden Horseshoe (No 34), The Green Lobster (No 43), the Two Suns (No 47) and the White Swan (No 49). Two magnificent baroque mansions, the Thun-Hohenstein Palace (No 20) and the Morzin Palace (No 5) are now the Italian and Romanian embassies. Nerudova leads eventually to Prague Castle, a wonderful vantage point from which to view the city.

4C Nerudova, Malá Strana Cafés (£), restaurants (££–£££) 12, 20, 22, 23 to Malostranské náměstí

NOVÝ SVĚT (NEW WORLD)

Nový Svět is a country lane of quaint cottages dating back to the 17th century. Look out for U zletého noha (At the Golden Griffin, No 1), where the astronomers Tycho Brahe and Johannes Kepler once lived and U zlaté hrušky (At the Golden Pear, No 3), now one of Prague's finest restaurants.

www.uzlatehrusky.cz

2D Nový Svět, Hradčany Restaurant (£££) 22, 23 to Pohořelec

PETŘÍNSKÉ SADY (PETŘÍN HILL)

Petřín Hill, where pagans once made sacrifices to their gods and medieval monarchs executed their enemies, is today a restful haven with panoramic views of the city. Crowning the summit is the baroque Church of St Lawrence; the ceiling fresco here depicts the founding of an earlier church in 991 on the site of a pagan shrine. The 60m-high (197ft) Observation Tower, modelled on the Eiffel Tower in Paris, was built for the Jubilee Exhibition of 1891, along with the Mirror Maze and a diorama depicting a battle between the Czechs and the Swedes for control of the Charles Bridge in 1648. Encircling the hill is the Hunger Wall, built in 1360 by Charles IV to provide employment in a time of famine. Further down the hill is the Observatory and Planetarium.

4A Petřínské sady, Malá Strana Tower: 257 320 112 All attractions: May–Aug daily 10–10; Apr, Sep 10–7; Oct 10–6; Nov–Mar Sat–Sun 10–5 Restaurant (£££) Funicular 6, 9, 12, 22, 23 to Újezd

PRAŽSKÝ HRAD

See pages 44–45.

ŠTERNBERSKÝ PALÁC

See pages 48–49.

STRAHOVSKÝ KLÁŠTER

See pages 50–51.

a walk through the Lesser Quarter

From Malostranská metro station take Valdštejnská to Valdštejnské náměstí.

Valdštejnské náměstí is named after the Imperial commander, Albrecht von Valdstein, whose palace straddles the east side (➤ 126–127). Behind the Ledebour Palace (No 3) are two attractive terraced gardens (open to the public), hugging the slopes below Prague Castle.

Take Tomásská to Malostranské náměstí. Walk along the east side of the square to Karmelitská.

Before crossing to Malostranské náměstí, stop to admire Dientzenhofer's baroque church, St Thomas's (➤ 114). The lower part of the square was once the site of a gallows and pillory. Now café tables spill onto the pavement outside the Town Hall.

Leave the square by Karmelitská and continue past Tržiště to the Church of Our Lady Victorious (➤ 114) which contains the celebrated statue of Il Bambino di Praga.

On the corner of Tržiště you pass the Vrtba Palace, which has a delightful terraced garden, constructed around 1720.

Cross Karmelitska and turn left down Harantova. Walk through Maltézské náměstí (➤ 119) and turn right onto Velkopřevorské náměstí, which leads down to the river.

Beyond the Lennon Wall (➤ 118) and the approach to the Vltava is a little bridge crossing the Čertovka (Devil's Stream). On your left is the waterwheel of the Grand Prior's Mill, which, in common with much of the area, belonged to the Order of the Knights of Malta.

Turn right and follow the river to most Legií, where you can catch a tram back to the centre.

Distance 2km (1 mile)
Time 2hours without stops
Start point Ⓜ Malostranská ✚ D6
End point most Legií ✚ A6 🚋 6, 9, 22, 23
Lunch U Malého Glena (£££) ✉ Karmelitská 23, Malá Strana
☎ 257 531 717; www.malyglen.cz

TROJSKÝ ZÁMEK (TROJA CHÂTEAU)

Count Wenceslas Šternberg cut a swathe through the royal hunting grounds in order to build his version of Versailles at Stromovka. Work began on the striking red-and-white château around 1679. The palace itself is modelled on an Italian villa, but after the death of the original architect, responsibility for the project passed into the hands of a Frenchman, Jean-Baptiste Mathey. To honour the architect's intentions, it is necessary to approach the château from the south, where the formal French garden, restored in the 1980s, leads to an elaborate staircase decorated with heroic statues representing the 'gigantomachia' – the epic struggle between the Gods of Olympus and the Titans. The château apartments now house 19th-century Czech paintings. Most of the ceiling paintings are by an Italian artist, Francesco Marchetti, but for the Grand Hall the count turned to the Flemish painter, Abraham Godyn. His frescoes are Šternberg's effusive tribute to his Habsburg masters, notably Leopold I, whose triumph over the Ottomans at the gates of Vienna is symbolized by a Turk tumbling from the painting.

www.ghmp.cz

25S (off map) U Trojského zámku 1, Troja, Praha 7 283 851 614 Apr–Oct Tue–Sun 10–6; Nov–Mar Sat–Sun 10–5 Moderate Bus 112 from Nádraží Holešovice

VALDŠTEJNSKÝ PALÁC A SADY (WALLENSTEIN PALACE AND GARDENS)

The Imperial General, Albrecht of Wallenstein (1583–1634), was a swashbuckling figure who amassed a tremendous fortune before succumbing to a blow from the assassin's axe. High-walled gardens were laid out in front of the palace by Niccolo Sebregondi between 1624 and 1630. The ceiling of the triple-arched *salla terrena*, designed in the Italian Renaissance style by Giovanni

Pieronni, is decorated with scenes from the Trojan Wars. An avenue of bronze sculptures by Adam de Vries leads from the pavilion (these are copies: the originals were taken by the Swedes during the Thirty Years' War). At the far end of the garden is the Riding School, now an exhibition hall.

www.senat.cz

5D Valdštejnské náměstí 4, Malá Strana 257 071 111 Sat–Sun 10–5 Free Malostranská 12, 20, 22, 23

VELETRŽNÍ PALÁC

See pages 54–55.

VÝSTAVÍŠTĚ – MORSKÝ SVĚT (EXHIBITION GROUND – SEAWORLD)

The Exhibition Ground in Letná Park dates from 1891 and has splendid art nouveau pavilions (➤ 117). Here also is Seaworld, a vast exhibition space devoted to the life of the deep. There are 50 tanks, containing more than 150 species of salt and freshwater fish from all over the world and a huge coral cave, constructed with American help in 2003. State-of-the-art technology replicates the natural environment with specially sensitized lighting, while microprocessor-driven water pumps simulate high and low tides.

www.morsky-svet.cz

27R Výstavište, Holešovice, Praha 7 5, 12, 14, 15, 17 to Výstaviště

ZLATÁ ULIČKA (GOLDEN LANE)

This row of colourful little cottages, built hard against the walls of Prague Castle, originally provided homes for the archers of the Castle Guard. During the 17th century the palace goldsmiths moved into the area, giving the street its present name. Golden Lane gradually fell into decline and was little better than a slum when Franz Kafka was living with his sister at No 22 during the winter of 1916–17. Today souvenir shops occupy the cottages.

5D Zlatá ulička, Pražský hrad, Hradčany Apr–Oct daily 9–5; Nov–Mar daily 9–4 Inexpensive Cafés (£) Malostranská 22

HOTELS

Hotel Kampa Garden (£££)

This 3-star hotel is in an historic building on the canal on Kampa Island, beside the water-wheel of Velkopřevorský Mill.

✉ U Sovových mlýnů 9, Malá Strana ☎ 233 920 118; www.hotelsprague.cz/kampagarden 🚋 12, 20, 22, 23 to Malostranské náměstí

Savoy (£££)

One of Prague's leading hotels, the Savoy is only a stone's throw from Hradčany. The rooms are well appointed and there's a reassuringly unhurried ambience.

✉ Kepelrova 6, Hradčany ☎ 224 302 430; www.hotel-savoy.cz 🚋 22, 23

Sax (£)

This sparkling clean, 3-star, 22-room hotel is tucked down a side street of Nerudova, the steep street leading to the castle.

✉ Janský vrsek 3, Malá Strana ☎ 257 531 268; www.sax.com 🚋 12, 20, 22, 23 to Malostranské náměstí

U Tří Pštrosů (£££)

Once the centre of a flourishing trade in feathers, 'At the Three Ostriches' is a charming hostelry next to Charles Bridge, just near Malostranské náměstí. The restaurant has a deservedly good reputation offering some excellent fish dishes.

✉ Dražického náměstí 12, Malá Strana ☎ 257 288 888; www.utripstrosu.cz 🚇 Malostranská

RESTAURANTS AND CAFÉS

Bohemia Bagel (£)

A friendly self-service café where you can get freshly baked bagels and a wide range of bagel sandwiches. There's also a good selection of soup, eggs and bacon, quiches, brownies and cookies.

✉ Újezd 16, Malá Strana ☎ 257 310 694; www.bohemiabagel.cz 🚋 12, 22, 23 to Újezd

Café Savoy (££)
A beautifully restored belle-époque café from 1893, just off the river, that serves a full breakfast, lunch and dinner menu.
✉ Vítězná 5, Smíchov, Praha 5 ☎ 257 311 562; www.ambi.cz 🚋 9, 22, 23 to Zborovská

Caffè-Ristorante Italia (££)
Traditional Italian specialities are served in this bright, modern restaurant on one of the loveliest streets in Prague.
✉ Nerudova 17, Hradčany ☎ 257 532 818 🚋 22, 23

Cantina (££)
If you're craving a *burrito*, *fajita* or *enchilada*, this is one of the best places in Prague to satisfy your appetite. It gets very busy at dinner so be prepared to wait unless you call ahead.
✉ Újezd 38, Malá Strana ☎ 257 317 173 🚋 9, 22, 23 to Újezd

Cowboys (£££)
Cowboys is Prague's newest restaurant from the Kampa group and is modelled after an American steakhouse, serving a range of char-broiled steaks and fresh fish. The winter garden tucked under the castle may be one of the loveliest dining areas in Prague.
✉ Nerudova 40, Malá Strana ☎ 257 535 050; www.kampagroup.com
🚋 12, 22, 23 to Malostranské náměstí

David (£££)
This stylish restaurant serving reinvented traditional Bohemian dishes gets very busy, so book ahead.
✉ Tržiště 21/611, Malá Strana ☎ 257 533 109; www.restaurant-david.cz
Ⓜ Malostranská 🚋 12, 20, 22, 23 to Malostranské náměstí

Gitane's (££)
A pretty, cosy little restaurant serving Croatian and Balkan specialities, including *čevapčiči* and *burek*.
✉ Tržiště 7, Malá Strana ☎ 257 530 163; www.gitanes.cz 🚋 12, 22, 23 to Malostranské náměstí

Hungarian Grotto (£)
Superb goulash, beef Budapest-style and many more spicy Hungarian specialities – they don't skimp on the paprika here. Live violin music makes the atmosphere festive.
Tomášská 12, Malá Strana 257 532 344 12, 22, 23 to Malostranské náměstí

Haveli (£££)
Not many Indian restaurants can boast this beautiful cellar setting. Good, if expensive, regional dishes including a respectable number of vegetarian offerings. Voted best Indian restaurant in Prague by the local English-language newspaper.
Dejvická 6, Dejvice, Praha 6 233 344 800; www.haveli.cz
Hradčanská

Kampa Park (£££)
This is a lovely restaurant overlooking the Vltava that specializes in lobster and game.
Na Kampě 8b, Malá Strana 296 826 102; www.kampagroup.com
Malostranská 12, 20, 22, 23 to Malostranské náměstí

Malý Buddha (£)
This is a soothing place to have lunch and serves simple Vietnamese, vegetarian-friendly food. Take some time out from sightseeing and linger over a steaming pot of tea from the wide selection available.
Úvoz 46, Hradčany 220 513 894

Pálffy Palác (££)
An elegant and upmarket palace restaurant. Book well in advance.
Valstětjnská 14, Malá Strana 257 530 522 Malostranská 22,23

Saté (£)
A small Indonesian restaurant near the castle serving spicy chicken, veg and meat dishes – perfect for lunch after sightseeing.
Pohořelec 3, Hradčany 220 514 552 22

U Maltézských Rytířů (££)

A lovely, old-world restaurant in Malá Strana. Delicious Czech cuisine with the emphasis on game, although salmon and other fish are also on the menu. Book ahead for a table in the 14th-century Gothic cellar.

✉ Prokopská 10, Malá Strana ☎ 257 530 075 🚌 12, 22, 23

U Vladaře (£££)

Located in Maltézské náměstí, this expensive but excellent restaurant specializes in old Prague favourites: leg of boar in garlic and juniper berries, roast goose with cabbage dumplings.

✉ Maltézské náměstí 10, Malá Strana ☎ 257 534 121; www.uvladare.cz
🚌 12, 22, 23 to Malostranské náměstí

SHOPPING

SPECIALITY SHOPPING

Capriccio

This store boasts the largest selection of sheet music in Prague: more than 10,000 items in all, including jazz and classical scores – also CDs.

✉ Újezd 15, Smíchov, Praha 5 ☎ 257 320 165 🚌 12, 22, 23

ENTERTAINMENT

DISCOS, CLUBS AND BARS

Bar Bar

This small, friendly bar situated in a cellar near the river in Malá Strana is a cosy little place, serving drinks and everything from bar snacks to main meals.

✉ Všehrdova 17, Malá Strana ☎ 257 312 246; www.bar-bar.cz
🚇 Malostranská 🚌 9,12, 22, 23 to Újezd

Mecca

Outside the central Prague area, this ultra-cool multi-level club has several theme rooms and won the vote for best dance music in town for a several years running.

✉ U průhonu 3, Holšovice, Praha 7 ☎ 283 870 522; www.mecca.cz
🚇 Vlatvská, then tram 15 to Dělnická

Josefov Area

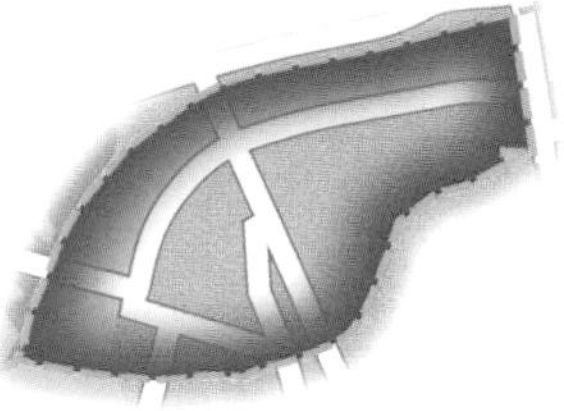

Josefov, the Old Jewish Quarter, is a compact area that stretches from Old Town Square up to Anežský klášter (Convent of St Agnes) and out to the Rudolfinum. Named in honour of Emperor Joseph II, 'Joseph's Town' retains the compact feel of the Jewish ghetto which during the late 18th century housed more than 12,000 people, although the city's current Jewish community numbers less than 3,000.

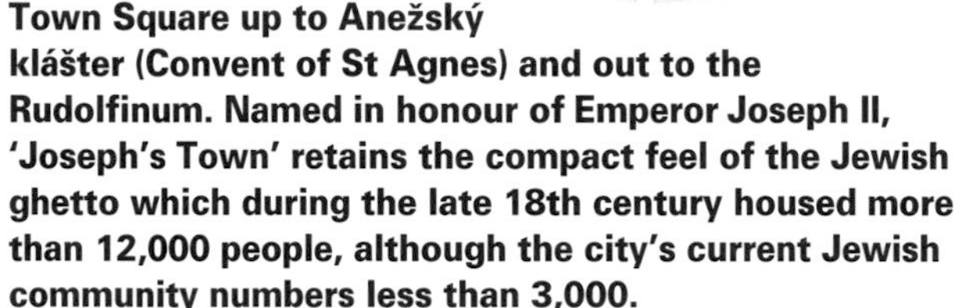

Like the Marais in Paris, Prague's Jewish quarter is now a neighbourhood of high rents, exclusive shops and expensive restaurants. Dominating the area are the beautiful Starý židovský hřbitov (Old Jewish Cemetery) and Staronová synagogá (Old-New Synagogue). On Maiselova Street you will find more synagogues and near to Pařížská třída (Paris Boulevard) is the Spanish Synagogue.

ANEŽSKÝ KLÁŠTER (ST AGNES CONVENT)

The convent was founded in 1234 by Agnes, sister of King Wenceslas I. St Agnes introduced the Order of Poor Clares into Bohemia and was the first abbess. Completed by the end of the 14th century and sacked by the Hussites in the 15th, the convent was eventually dissolved in 1782. An ambitious restoration programme was completed in the 1990s. The most impressive building is the Church of the Holy Saviour, an outstanding example of early Gothic architecture. Look out for the capitals, which are highly decorated with reliefs showing the rulers of the Přemyslid dynasty. During restoration, the burial place of some of these kings and queens was unearthed, including the tomb of King Wenceslas in the Church of St Francis (which is now used as a concert venue).

The convent houses an excellent exhibition of medieval art from Bohemia and Central Europe (1200–1550). Among the highlights are works by two artists active in the reign of Charles IV: the Master of the Vyšší Brod Altar and Master Theodoric, whose lustrous portraits of the saints were intended for the chapel of Karlštejn Castle.

9E · U milosrdných 17, Josefov · 224 810 628 · Tue–Sun 10–6 · Moderate · Staroměstská, Náměstí Republiky · 5, 17, 14, 26

EXPOZICE FRANZE KAFKY (FRANZ KAFKA EXHIBITION)

A sculpted relief marks the site of the house where Franz Kafka was born in 1883. Only the doorway of the original building, At the Tower, remains following a fire in 1887. Kafka's love-hate relationship with Prague is reflected in his novels *The Trial* and *The Castle*, where the city's menacing presence looms over the characters. Kafka died in 1924. A photographic exhibition of his life can be found on the ground floor.

8C Náměstí Franze Kafky 3, Staré Město 222 321 675 Tue–Fri 10–6, Sat 10–5 Inexpensive Café (£), restaurants (££–£££) near by Staroměstská

JOSEFOV

See pages 38–39.

KLAUSOVÁ SYNAGOGA (KLAUSEN SYNAGOGUE)

A number of religious schools and other buildings known as *klausen* were cleared away after the great fire of 1689 to make way for this early baroque synagogue. The fine interior, with barrel-vaulted roof, stuccoed ceiling ornamentation and stained-glass windows, has been restored and now contains an exhibition on local Jewish customs and traditions, including old Hebrew manuscripts and prints, beautifully worked Torah ornaments, skull caps embroidered in satin and velvet, bronze Hanukkah lamps and a curious wooden alms box

(*c*1800) with a supplicating hand and arm. The marble Holy Ark, made in 1696 at the expense of Samuel Openheim, has also been restored.

8D U starého hřbitova 3a, Josefov Jewish Museum: 222 317 191 Apr–Oct Sun–Fri 9–6; Nov–Mar Sun–Fri 9–4.30. Closed Sat and Jewish hols Moderate Staroměstská 17, 18

KOSTEL SVATÉHO MIKULÁŠ (ST NICHOLAS'S CHURCH)

This beautifully proportioned baroque masterpiece was designed by the prolific architect Kilián Dientzenhofer in 1732 and completed three years later. (The sculptures of saints are by Antonin Braun.) St Nicholas (➤ 71) stands on the site of a much older Gothic church. When, in the spirit of the Enlightenment, the Emperor Joseph II evicted the Benedictines later in the 18th century, on the grounds that they were not performing a useful function, the church was used as a warehouse and fell into disrepair. It was saved during World War I when the commander of the occupying garrison invited local artists to restore Kosmas Asam's frescoes of saints Nicholas and Benedict in the dome. In other respects the building lacks the exuberance of baroque ornamentation.

Since 1920 St Nicholas has belonged to the Czech Reformed (Hussite) Church and is regularly used for concerts; the church has a 2,500-pipe organ.

9C Staroměstské náměstí, Staré Město Mon 12–4, Tue–Sat 10–4, Sun 10.30 (Mass), 12–3, also for concerts Free Cafés (£), restaurants (££–£££) near by Staroměstská

MAISELOVA SYNAGOGA (MAISEL SYNAGOGUE)

Originally a Renaissance temple, built in 1591 for Mayor Mordechai Maisel, financier to Emperor Rudolph II, the synagogue has a beautifully restored interior, which preserves some of the 16th-century stone carving.

The building now houses an exhibition of sacred religious objects, including items associated with the Torah. This consists of the five books of Moses, handwritten on rolls of parchment by scribes. By tradition the rollers would be elaborately decorated with filials, shields and crowns, superbly wrought in silver or brass and often gilded or encrusted with jewels. Examples of the richly embroidered mantles in which the Torah was wrapped are also on display in the synagogue, along with other items. But the most unusual exhibit is an enormous glass beaker, made between 1783 and 1784 for the Prague Burial Society and painted with a procession of men and women dressed in funereal black.

8C Maiselova 10, Josefov Jewish Museum: 222 317 191
Apr–Oct Sun–Fri 9–6; Nov–Mar 9–4.30. Closed Sat and Jewish hols
Moderate Staroměstská 17, 18

MUZEUM UMĚLECKOPRŮMYSLOVÉ (MUSEUM OF DECORATIVE ARTS)

Once housed in the Rudolfinum, the museum moved to Josef Schulz's neo-Renaissance building in 1901, and boasts a rich collection of Czech and European applied arts. The collection of Bohemian glass dates back to the Renaissance and is outstanding, as are Venetian and medieval exhibits. There are selections of Meissen and Sèvres porcelain, exquisite majolica tableware from Urbino and Delft and beautifully inlaid cabinets, bureaux and escritoires, from baroque to Biedermeier. The museum shop sells a wide range of publications and souvenirs.

www.upm.cz

8D 17 listopadu 2, Josefov 251 093 111 Tue 10–7, Wed–Sun 10–6 Inexpensive Café (£) Staroměstská 17, 18

NÁMĚSTÍ JANA PALACHA (JAN PALACH SQUARE)

'Red Army Square' was renamed after the 1989 Velvet Revolution in honour of Jan Palach, the 21-year-old philosophy student who burned himself to death in January 1969 as a protest against the Soviet occupation of Czechoslovakia. The authorities were unmoved but more than 800,000 people joined the funeral procession to Olšanské cemetery, where his remains were laid to rest. On the east side of the square is the philosophy building of Charles University, where Palach attended lectures: on the lower left-hand corner of the façade is a small bronze death mask by Olbran Zoubek.

7D Náměstí Jana Palacha, Josefov Free Café (£) near by Staroměstská 17, 18

OBŘADNÍ SÍŇ (CEREMONIAL HALL)

The former Ceremonial Hall of the Prague Burial Society was once used for Jewish burial rites. It now houses a permanent exhibition on Jewish customs and traditions, with particular emphasis on the themes of illness and death.

8D U starého hřbitova, Josefov Jewish Museum: 222 317 191 Apr–Oct Sun–Fri 9–6; Nov–Mar 9–4.30. Closed Sat and Jewish hols Staroměstská Moderate 17, 18

PINKASOVA SYNAGOGA (PINKAS SYNAGOGUE)

First mentioned in 1492, this synagogue was founded by Rabbi Pinkas and enlarged in 1535. A women's gallery and council hall were added in the 17th century. Now a Holocaust memorial, its walls have been painstakingly painted with the names of the 77,297 Bohemian and Moravian Jews who perished in Nazi death camps during World War II. (The original paintings were erased by the Communists when they closed the building in 1968, ostensibly to prevent flood damage.) During excavations, a medieval ritual bath was discovered in the basement, evidence that the site was a Jewish place of worship long before the time of Rabbi Pinkas.

The upper floor of the synagogue houses a moving collection of drawings by some of the 15,000 children who were confined at the Terezín concentration camp. Mrs Friedl Dicker-Brandeis (1898–1944), an artist and graduate of the Bauhaus, organised art classes which functioned as a kind of therapy for the children: their drawings often depicted their transportation to Terezín, their memories of home and their dreams of returning to their families.

8D Široká 3, Josefov Jewish Museum: 222 317 191 Apr–Oct Sun–Fri 9–6; Nov–Mar 9–4.30. Closed Sat and Jewish hols Moderate Café (£), restaurant (££) near by Staroměstská 17, 18

RUDOLFINUM

One of Prague's leading cultural venues, the Rudolfinum is also a fine example of neo-Renaissance architecture. It was designed by Josef Zítek and Josef Schulz in 1876 and named in honour of the Austrian crown prince, Rudolph of Habsburg. During World War II it was used as the German Army HQ and before that (1918–38) it housed the first Czechoslovak parliament. Concert-goers will come to know the Dvořák Hall, home of the Czech Philharmonic orchestra (chamber concerts and recitals are held in the 'small hall'). The Galerie Rudolfinum is used for art shows and events.

www.rudolfinum.cz

7D Alšovo nábřeží 12, Josefov 227 059 227 Gallery: Tue–Sun 10–6 Moderate Staroměstská 17, 18

STARONOVÁ SYNAGOGA (OLD-NEW SYNAGOGUE)

Founded around 1270, the Old-New Synagogue is the oldest in Europe and is still open for worship. A typical Gothic building with a double nave, its most unusual feature is the five-ribbed vaulting of the main hall, unique in Bohemian architecture. Other details to look out for are the stepped brick gables on the exterior, the grape clusters and vine leaf motifs above the entrance portal and the medieval furnishings, including stone pews. There are 13th-century Gothic carvings in the tympanum above the Holy Ark, and the iron lattice enclosing the *almenor* or *bimah* (the tribune from where the Torah is read) dates from the late 15th century. During the sabbath (Saturday) service seven members of the congregation join in the reading. Suspended between two of the pillars is a large red flag embroidered with the Star of David and the traditional Jewish cap. It was presented to the community in 1648 by the Emperor Ferdinand in appreciation of its contribution to the Thirty Years' War.

8D Červená 2, Josefov Apr–Oct Sun–Thu 9–6, Fri 9–5; Nov–Mar Sun–Thu 9–4.30, Fri 9–2. Closed Sat and Jewish hols Moderate Restaurant (££) near by Staroměstská 17, 18

STARÝ ŽIDOVSKÝ HŘBITOV (OLD JEWISH CEMETERY)

One of the oldest Jewish burial grounds in Europe, the Old Jewish Cemetery was founded in the early 15th century: the earliest grave, belonging to Rabbi Avigdor Kara, dates from 1439. There are approximately 12,000 tombstones sprouting obliquely from the earth like broken and decaying teeth. Beneath them lie more than 100,000 bodies, buried layer upon layer in the confined space. The cemetery closed in 1787. This was the last resting place of many prominent members of the Jewish community, including Rabbi Jehuda Löw (1609), legendary inventor of the Golem, the mayor and philanthropist Mordechai Maisel (1601) and the renowned scholar Rabbi David Openheim (1736). The earliest headstones are of sandstone and have plain inscriptions, but from the 17th century they are decorated with carved marble reliefs indicating the trade or status of the deceased – for example, a pair of scissors for a tailor.

8D U starého hřbitova, Josefov Jewish Museum: 222 317 191 Apr–Oct Sun–Fri 9–6; Nov–Mar 9–4.30. Closed Sat and Jewish hols Moderate Staroměstská 17, 18

HOTELS

Hotel Casa Marcello (££)

This small hotel is located in a restored 13th-century building which was once part of St Agnes convent.

✉ Rásnovka 783, Josefov ☎ 222 310 260; www.casa-marcello.cz 🚌 8, 14 to Dlouhá třída

Maximilian (££)

Not far from the Old Town Square, this plush, Austrian-run boutique hotel is on a quiet square facing a church.

✉ Haštalská 14, Josefov ☎ 225 303 110; www.maximilianhotel.com 🚇 Náměstí Republiky 🚌 8, 14 to Dlouhá třída

RESTAURANTS

Arzenal (£££)

Renowned Czech architect Bořek Šípek's stunning glass shop-front and gallery paves the way for a superb Thai restaurant that has attracted numerous celebrity visitors. Good fish, curries and vegetarian dishes.

✉ Valentinská 11, Staré Město ☎ 224 814 099; www.arzenal.cz 🚇 Staroměstská

Blinis Bar (£)

Just away form the Old Town Square, this Jewish restaurant serves warming blinis and a good range of Russian vodka.

✉ Maiselova 16, Josefov ☎ 224 812 463

Kolkovna (£–££)

A lively pub-restaurant with a smartly designed interior, excellent traditional Czech menu and Pilsner Urquell straight from the tank.

✉ V Kolkovně 8, Josefov ☎ 224 819 701; www.kolkovna-group.cz 🚇 Staroměstská

Pizzeria Rugantino (££)

A good lunchtime stopover for visitors to Josefov: the wood-oven pizzas here are enormously satisfying.

✉ Dušní 4, Josefov ☎ 222 318 172; www.rugantino.cz 🚌 17, 18

Café La Veranda (£££)

Great food and a stylish interior is winning this restaurant rave reviews from critics and diners.

✉ Elišky Krásnohorská 2, Josefov ☎ 224 814 733; www.laveranda.cz
🚇 Staroměstská

SHOPPING

CLOTHING, JEWELLERY AND ACCESSORIES

Bohéme

Specialist in designer Czech knitwear; also sells attractively priced leather goods and interesting accessories.

✉ Dušní 8, Josefov ☎ 224 813 840 🚇 Staroměstská

Fabergé

Czech representative of the world-renowned Russian jewellers, specializing in ornamental eggs; also stocks traditional jewellery.

✉ Pařížská 15, Josefov ☎ 222 323 085 🚇 Staroměstská

ENTERTAINMENT

BARS

Ocean Drive

A stylish nightspot specializing in fancy cocktails.

✉ V Kolkovně 7, Josefov ☎ 224 819 089 🚇 Staroměstská

Tretter's Bar

A classy cocktail lounge graced by glitterati, with a 1930s feel.

✉ V Kolkovne 3. Josefov ☎ 224 811 165; www.tretters.cz

THEATRES AND CONCERT HALLS

Národní Divadlo Marionet (National Marionette Theatre)

Puppets and costumed actors perform classical operas as well as some lighter fare. Performances usually begin at 8pm.

✉ Žatecká 1, Staré Město ☎ 224 901 448; www.narodni-divadlo.cz
🚇 Staroměstská

Rudolfinum

See page 142.

Nové Město and Beyond

The New Town was founded in the 14th century and is now the commercial and administrative heart of the city with new, modern buildings rubbing shoulders with old. It fills the area from the avenues of Na příkopě and Národní south by the Vltava River down to the dramatic ramparts of Vyšehrad. East of this is Vinohrady, a leafy neighbourhood filled with restaurants and parks.

Even first-time visitors will probably have heard of Wenceslas Square or Václavské náměstí. To call it a square is misleading; it's actually a long boulevard that is crowned at the top by a massive statue of St Wenceslas on horseback, and the majestic National Museum. Both sides of the 'square' are

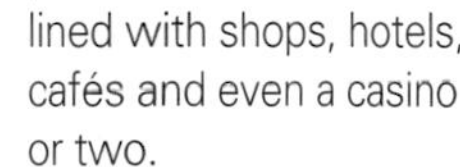

lined with shops, hotels, cafés and even a casino or two.

The Národní divadlo (National Theatre) and the Café Slavia, once the haunt of dissidents in communist times, are both highlights of Nové Město and are on Národní třída.

CHRÁM PANNY MARIE SNĚŽNÉ (OUR LADY OF THE SNOWS)

Founded in 1347 by Charles IV, Our Lady of the Snows was to have been the largest church in Prague – 40m (131ft) high and 110m (360ft) long – but the outbreak of the Hussite wars interrupted work on the building. In 1603 the completed choir was restored to the Franciscans and given a baroque face-lift and a new vaulted ceiling. All that remains of the 14th-century church are the crumbling pediment over the north gateway and the pewter font. The Franciscan Gardens are now a public park.

www.pms.ofm.cz

9A Jungmannovo náměstí 18, Nové Město 224 916 100 Daily 7–7. Mass: Mon–Fri 7am, 8am and 6pm, Sat 8am and 6pm, Sun 9am, 10.15am, 11.30am and 6pm. Evening concerts: tickets at the door Free Můstek

DVOŘÁKA ANTONÍN MUZEUM (DVORAK MUSEUM)

This beautiful baroque mansion, built by Kilián Dientzenhofer between 1717 and 1720 for a prominant Czech nobleman, acquired its present name, Vila Amerika, in the 19th century – there was an eating house of that name near by. It is therefore entirely appropriate that the building now honours the composer of the 'New World' symphony, Antonín Dvořák (1841–1904). Unfortunately, the palatial interior, with partly restored frescoes by Johann Schlor, is not really suitable for such an intimate exhibition. The exhibits, spread over two floors, include autographed scores, photographs, busts and portraits, correspondence with fellow musicians (the composers Brahms and Tchaikovsky, and the German conductor Hans von Bulöw, were among Dvořák's friends and admirers) and a number of personal effects including his viola, Bible and spectacles. The first floor is also used for concerts.

www.nm.cz

20K Ke Karlovu 20, Nové Město 224 918 013 Tue–Sun 10–5 Inexpensive IP Pavlova 4, 10, 16, 22, 23

KOSTEL SVATÉHO CYRILA A METODĚJE (CHURCH OF SAINTS CYRIL AND METHODIUS)

A plaque on the bullet-scarred wall of this Orthodox cathedral commemorates the Free Czech paratroopers who died here on 18 June 1942, after taking part in the assassination of the Nazi Governor of Bohemia and Moravia, Reinhard Heydrich. Members of the Czech Orthodox community hid them in the crypt, but they were discovered, and committed suicide rather than fall into enemy hands. Saints Cyril and Methodius was designated a National Memorial to the victims of the Heydrich Terror.

www.pravoslavnacirkev.cz

18L Resslova 9, Nové Město 224 920 686 Apr–Oct Tue–Sun 10–5; Nov–Mar Tue–Sun 10–4. Crypt by appointment only Inexpensive Karlovo náměstí 4, 6, 10, 14, 16, 22, 23, 24

MUZEUM HLAVNÍHO MĚSTA PRAHY (CITY OF PRAGUE MUSEUM)

One of the three historic buildings that make up the City of Prague Museum, Hlavni Budova na Florenci charts the history of the city and includes exhibits which range from the earliest times to the 20th century. Among the various household items on display are slippers, combs and a 14th-century wash-tub, as well as pottery and coins. The medieval craft guilds are represented in displays of tools, signs and seals, and by some fine examples of their workmanship, including a mural painting of 1406, originally executed for the House at the Golden Angel in Old Town Square. Weapons, model soldiers and cannons and the lock of the original Bethlehem Chapel door (➤ 84–85) are used to illustrate the Hussite period, and there is an impressive collection of statuary, notably a wooden *pietà* from the Týn Church (➤ 91) and a stone

Madonna which used to decorate the Oriel Chapel in the Old Town Hall (► 46–47). Another attraction is Antonín Langweil's ambitious model of 19th-century Prague, which can be illuminated to show different areas of the city. The Muller Villa and Vyton building make up the museum complex.

www.muzeumprahy.cz

12D Na poříčí 52, Karlín, Praha 8 224 212 966 Daily 9–9 Inexpensive Florenc 8, 24

MUZEUM KOMUNISMU (MUSEUM OF COMMUNISM)

As a modern visitor to Prague it's all too easy to forget that for more than 40 years (1948–89) the Czech Republic was an occupied country within the Soviet bloc, a client state adhering to the prevailing Communist ideology. Through photographs, household ephemera, agricultural machinery, military hardware, propaganda posters, reproductions of bare food shelves and 'Young Pioneer' classrooms, the exhibition 'Dreams, Reality and Nightmare of Communism' is an intriguing introduction to life in a satellite Soviet state and a sobering reminder of what the Czech people had to endure. An interrogation room from the 1950s show-trial era is chillingly reproduced, and the persistent ring of a black telephone is a suitably eerie touch.

www.muzeumkommunismu.cz

10B Savarin Palace, Na příkopě 10, Nové Město (first floor, same as casino) 224 212 966 Daily 8am–9pm Moderate Můstek

MUZEUM ALPHONSE MUCHY (MUCHA MUSEUM)

This museum allows you an opportunity to discover the work of one of the great masters of art nouveau, Alphonse Mucha (1860–1939). Mucha began his career in 1887, shortly after studying at the Academy of Arts in Munich, when he found work as a set painter and decorator in Vienna and Paris. His most famous early illustrations were the posters designed for the French actress Sarah Bernhardt. He settled in Prague in 1910, having spent several years teaching.

Other examples of his work can be seen in Obecní dům, the National Gallery and the Art and Industry Museum. The collection is a representative cross-section of works from the Mucha Foundation: paintings, drawings, lithographs, pastels, sculptures, photographs and personal memorabilia. The museum shop sells a range of souvenirs and gorgeous poster reproductions with the elegant Mucha motif.

www.mucha.cz

10B Panská 7, Nové Město 221 451 333 Daily 10–6 Moderate Můstek 5, 9 to Jindřišská

NA PŘÍKOPĚ (ON THE MOAT)

This busy, pedestrian-only street takes its name from the moat that once formed a boundary between the Old and New Towns. Today it is one of Prague's major shopping thoroughfares, with some compelling architecture from the late 19th century, when a number of major banking houses established their offices here. Particularly impressive is No 18–20. Actually two buildings connected by a bridge, it was designed by Osvald Polívka and completed in 1896. An earlier building, No 10 on the south side, was designed by Kilián Ignac Dienzenhofer in 1743 and served as a casino then as it does now. The colourful mosaics in the lunettes are from cartoons by the Czech artist Mikoláš Aleš.

10B Na příkopě, Nové Město Free Cafés (£), restaurants (££) Můstek, Náměstí Republiky

NÁRODNÍ DIVADLO (NATIONAL THEATRE)

Partly funded by public donations, the founding of a National Theatre in this striking building represented the re-emergence of Czech nationalism in the mid-19th century. The foundation stone was laid in 1848, and when the almost completed theatre was destroyed by fire in 1881, more money was raised and a second National Theatre was finished in just two years. The design by Josef Schulz closely followed Josef Zítek's original.

The decoration was entrusted to a group of artists who became known as 'the generation of the National Theatre'. The loggia facing Národní has five arcades decorated with lunette paintings by Josef Tulka, while the attic contains statues by Bohuslav Schnirch, Antonin Wagner and Josef Myslbek. The interior is even more resplendent: in the portrait gallery, Myslbek sculpted bronze busts of Smetana and other contributors to Czech opera and drama, and Mikoláš Aleš, Adolf Liebscher and František Ženíšek filled the foyers with paintings. The stage curtain depicting the story of the National Theatre is by Voitěch Hynais.

www.narodni-divadlo.cz

7A Národní 2, Nové Město Box office: 224 901 377

Café-bar (££) Národní třída 6, 9, 17, 18, 22, 23 to Národní divadlo

Tours Sat–Sun 8.30–11am

NÁRODNÍ MUZEUM (NATIONAL MUSEUM)

This stolid neo-Renaissance building, crowned with a gilded dome, dominates Wenceslas Square. Serving up large but unimaginative helpings of natural history, mineralogy, palaeontology, zoology and anthropology, the museum is worth visiting for the richly decorated Ceremonial Hall and Pantheon. Statues of famous Czechs compete with historical wall paintings and allegories of Science, Art, Inspiration and Power, all commissioned from Bohemia's best 19th-century sculptors and painters.

www.nm.cz

21M Václavské náměstí 68, Nové Město 224 497 111 May–Sep daily 10–6; Oct–Apr daily 9–5. Closed first Tue every month Moderate Café (£) Muzeum 11

OBECNÍ DŮM (MUNICIPAL HOUSE)

One of Prague's most engaging art nouveau monuments, Obecní dům was conceived as a community centre with concert halls, assembly rooms, offices and cafés. Antonín Balšánek and Osvald Polívka won a competition for the design and it was completed in 1911. Each of the rooms has its own character, but there is overall unity in the stained-glass windows, inlaid floors, wrought-iron work and walls of polished wood or marble. Scarcely a Czech artist of the period failed to contribute to the interiors. The Smetana Concert Hall was decorated by Karel Špillar and Ladislav Šaloun; Alphonse Mucha was responsible for the Mayor's Salon. Špillar's large mosaic, *Homage to Prague*, on the façade, is also impressive.

www.obecnidum.cz

10C Náměstí Republiky 5, Nové Město 222 002 127; 222 002 101 Tours: moderate Café (£), restaurants (£££) Náměstí Republiky 5, 14, 26 Temporary exhibitions

PAMÁTNÍK 17 LISTOPADU 1989

In an arcade between Wenceslas Square and the National Theatre is a small plaque commemorating the incident that sparked the Velvet Revolution in 1989. On 17 November a large crowd, made up predominantly of students, headed towards Wenceslas Square from Vyšehrad, where they had been marking the 50th anniversary of the Nazi occupation. When they reached Národní they were confronted by riot police who charged, leaving hundreds severely beaten. Actors and theatre employees immediately called a strike, which led ultimately to the formation of Civic Forum.

8A Národní, Nové Město Free Cafés (£), restaurants (££–£££) near by Národní třída 6, 9, 18, 22, 23

POŠTOVNÍ MUZEUM (POSTAL MUSEUM)

This unusual museum boasts a colourful collection of postage stamps from Czechoslovakia, the Czech Republic and Europe. The backdrop is an exhibition on the history of communications in the region, using prints, old signs and other ephemera. There are also temporary exhibitions. The frescoes in the showroom are by the 19th-century artist, Josef Navrátil.

www.cpost.cz

10E Nové mlyny 2, Nové Město 222 312 006 Tue–Sun 9–5 Inexpensive Náměstí Republiky 5, 8, 14

PRAŠNÁ BRÁNA (POWDER GATE)

Work began on this sturdy Gothic tower in 1475, but was halted eight years later when rioting forced the king to flee the city. It still lacked a roof when Josef Mocker was asked to complete it in the 1870s. The gate acquired its name in the 17th century, when it was used to store gunpowder. Before then its functions had been ceremonial: coronation processions began here before moving off towards St Vitus's Cathedral.

10C Na příkopě, Nové Město 724 063 723 Apr–Oct daily 10–6 Moderate Náměstí Republiky 5, 14, 26

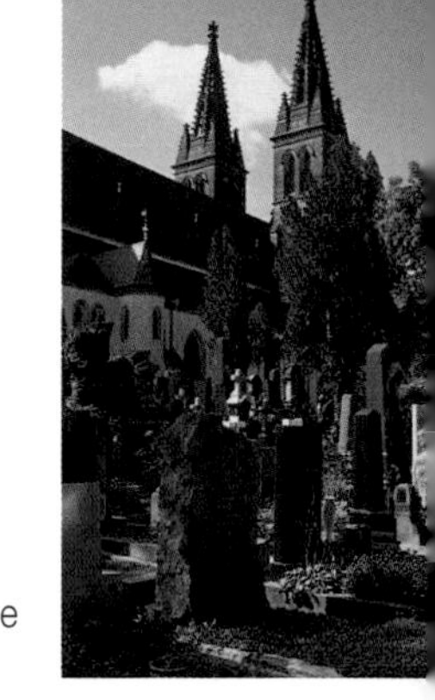

VÁCLAVSKÉ NÁMĚSTÍ

See pages 52–53.

VYŠEHRAD

The twin spires of Vyšehrad church are one of Prague's best known landmarks. The early history of this settlement is bound in legend surrounding the first dynasty of Czech rulers, the Přemyslids, who established a fortress on the rocky outcrop in the middle of the 10th century. Prince Vratislav II (1061–92) built a walled palace here, the Basilica of St Peter and St Paul and a chapter house. By the mid-12th century, Prague Castle began to take precedence, but Vyšehrad's value as a stronghold was noted by Charles IV, who reinforced the walls and made this the start of his coronation procession.

The elaborate Leopold Gate of 1670 leads into the main compound. Past St Martin's Rotunda is the Old Deanery, which stands on the site of a Romanesque basilica. Little remains of the early palaces, although from the terrace on the fortified walls there are views of 'Libuše's bath', actually a Gothic guard tower, as well as splendid vistas across the Vltava Valley. In the middle of the palace gardens is a medieval well – the statues by Josef Myslbek were removed from the Palacky Bridge after being damaged during a bombardment in 1945. The Church of St Peter and St Paul has been rebuilt many times, most recently in neo-Gothic style by Josef Mocker. In a side chapel is a medieval panel painting of the Virgin of the Rains, dating from 1350. Vyšehrad cemetery was founded in 1860 as a burial ground for Czech national heroes: the composers Antonín Dvořák and Bedřich Smetana, the artist Alphonse Mucha and the writer Karel Čapek are all buried here.

www.praha-vysehrad.cz

18G V pevnosti 5, Vyšehrad, Praha 2 241 410 348 Apr–Oct daily 9.30–6; Nov–Mar 9.30–5 Inexpensive Vyšehrad 7, 8, 24 to Albertov

HOTELS

Elysee (££)
Newly built hotel with a convenient location overlooking Wencelas Square. All 70 rooms are of generous size and some are adapted for visitors with disabilities.
Václavské náměstí 43, Nové Město 221 455 111; www.europehotels.cz Můstek

Hotel Adria (£££)
Hotel Adria is near the Franciscan Gardens and has excellent facilities, including satellite TV, bars and fitness centre.
Václavské náměstí 26, Nové Město 221 081 111; www.hoteladria.cz Můstek

Hotel Beranek (££)
Housed in a lovely classical building that used to be a bank, this new hotel has 80 fully equipped modern rooms.
Belehradská 110, Vinohrady, Praha 2 221 595 959; www.hotelberanek.cz IP Pavlova 4, 10, 16, 22, 23

Hotel Merkur (££)
This centrally located hotel has 54 sparkling-clean rooms, a generous breakfast and an outdoor patio for dining in summer.
Těšnov 9, Nové Město 226 201 910; www.ctg.cz/hotels/merkur Florenc

Hotel Pension City (£)
The rooms in this spotless and well-run pension are airy and spacious and a good buffet breakfast is included in the price.
Belgická 10, Vinohrady, Praha 2 222 521 606; www.hotelpensioncity.com Náměstí Míru 4, 10, 16, 22, 23

Pension U Suteru (£)
Tucked away on a quiet street, this spotless 14th-century pension has kept the Gothic architecture in its 10 double/deluxe rooms.
Palackého 4, Nové Město 233 920 118; www.hotelsprague.cz/usuteru Můstek 4, 6, 16, 22, 23 to Štěpánská

RESTAURANTS

Don Pedro's (££)

A cosy, festive restaurant near the river serving authentic Columbian food and cocktails.

Masarykovo nábřeží 2, Nové Město 224 923 505; www.donpedros.cz
Palackého náměstí

Dinitz (££)

In a soaring, art deco space, this restaurant serves an excellent international menu, starting with hearty breakfasts and ending with delicious dinners. After 10pm the scene picks up with a DJ.

Na poříčí 12, Nové Město 222 314 071; www.dinitz.cz

Dynamo (££)

A useful spot for lunch in a back-street location not far from the National Theatre. The modern Czech cuisine includes potato wedges, spicy chicken and peppered steak with corn on the cob.

Pštrossova 29, Nové Město 224 932 020 Národní třída

Grossetto (£)

Judging by the queues, this must be Prague's most popular pizza-pasta restaurant of the moment. The secret of its success probably lies in the uniformly generous helpings.

Francouzská 2, Vinohrady, Praha 2 224 252 778; www.grosseto.cz
Náměstí Míru 4, 10, 16, 22, 23

Jarmark (£)

Good-value, cafeteria-style restaurant in the Lucerna Passage. Appetizing salads, grills, stir-fries, pastries and fresh fruit.

Vodičkova 30, Nové Město (through Platyz passageway) 224 233 733
Můstek 3, 9, 14, 24

Kaaba (£)

A great place to rest from sightseeing, Kaaba has international coffees, teas and newspapers, as well as quality Czech wines.

Mánesova 20, Vinohrady, Praha 2 222 254 021 Jiřiho z Poděbrad
11 to Vinohradská tržnice

La Perle de Prague (£££)
Located in the arresting Tančící dům (also known as the 'dancing building'), this French restaurant has great views of the Vltava.
✉ Rašinovo nábřeží 80, Nové Město by Jiráskův bridge ☎ 221 984 160; www.laperle.cz Ⓜ Karlovo náměstí 🚋 3, 17, 21

Mozaika (££)
Hidden on a tree-lined street, Mozaika is heralded as one of the best places in Prague for a casual meal.
✉ Nitranská 13, Vinohrady, Praha 2 ☎ 224 253 011; www.restaurantmozaika.cz Ⓜ Jiřího z Poděbrad 🚋 11

Obecní dům (£–£££)
See page 155.

Pizzeria Kmotra (££)
This Italian cellar restaurant is something of an institution, and offers an extensive choice of wood-fired pizzas.
✉ V jirchářich 12, Nové Město ☎ 224 934 100 Ⓜ Národní třída 🚋 6, 9, 18, 22, 23

Rudý Baron (££)
The eye-catching décor of 'The Red Baron' pays tribute to the famous World War I flying ace. The large menu has something for everyone. Usually very busy, so dinner reservations are essential.
✉ Korunní 23, Vinohrady, Praha 2 ☎ 222 511 348; www.rudybaron.cz Ⓜ Náměstí Míru 🚋 4, 10, 16, 22, 23

Taverna Olympos (££)
A wonderful Greek taverna serving a wide range of national delicacies. Excellent *meze* menu. The large outdoor patio at the back is a treat in the summer. Book early.
✉ Kubelikova 9, Žižkov, Praha 3 ☎ 222 722 239; www.tavernaolympos.cz Ⓜ Jiřiho z Poděbrad 🚋 11

U Kalicha (£££)
See page 61.

Universal (££)

The atmosphere is cool French bistro but the cooking is more Czech-Mediterranean. Excellent salads, roasted meats and desserts.

✉ V Jirchářich 6, Nové Město ☎ 224 934 416 Ⓜ Národní třída 🚋 6, 9, 22, 23

SHOPPING

SPECIALITY SHOPS

The Globe Bookstore and Cafe

Founded in the 1990s, this legendary local institution offers a well-edited selection of Central and Eastern European fiction, an internet area and a café serving organic meals.

✉ Pštrossova 6, Nové Město ☎ 224 934 203; www.globebookstore.cz Ⓜ Staroměstská

JHB

A fascinating range of antiques and curios, including clocks and watches, silverware, porcelain figurines and paintings.

✉ Panská 1, Nové Město ☎ 222 245 836 Ⓜ Můstek

Knihkupectví Academia

A large bookstore with Czech, German, French and English fiction and nonfiction, and a large travel section. Have a coffee or a glass of wine on the second floor.

✉ Václavské náměstí 34, Nové Město ☎ 224 223 511 Ⓜ Můstek

FOOD AND DRINK

Cukrárna Simona

A small shop packed with sweets, chocolates and drinks such as *Becherovka* and *slivovice*, Balkan raki and Hungarian Tokay wine.

✉ Václavské náměstí 14, Nové Město ☎ 224 227 585 Ⓜ Můstek, Muzeum

Marks & Spencer

In a former communist-era bank, the top floor houses a gourmet food shop and relaxing café.

✉ Václavské náměstí 36, Nové Město ☎ 224 235 735 Ⓜ Můstek

ENTERTAINMENT

BARS

U Fleků

Czechs pride themselves on their beer and after a few of the dark Fleků beers brewed in this 12th-century building, you'll know why

✉ Křemencova 11, Nové Město ☎ 224 934 019; www.ufleku.cz
Ⓜ Národní třída

Radost FX

Easily the most famous club in the city. A vegetarian café at street level, a Moroccan-themed lounge in the back, and downstairs a hedonistic dance club that only gets going after midnight.

✉ Bélehradská 120, Vinohrady, Praha 2 ☎ 224 254 776; www.radostfx.cz

THEATRES AND CONCERT HALLS

Laterna Magika (Magic Lantern)

Dramatic performances combining drama, music, light, video and dance. Performances at 5 and 8pm.

✉ Národní 4, Nové Město ☎ 224 931 482; www.laternamagika.cz
Ⓜ Národní třída 🚋 9, 18, 22, 23 to Národní divadlo

Lucerna Music Bar

A two-level underground dance-and-band hall that has great energy and accoustics. One of the oldest concert halls in the city.

✉ Vodičkova 36, Nové Město ☎ 224 217 108; www.musicbar.cz Ⓜ Můstek
🚋 3, 9, 14 to Vodičkova

Smetanova síň (Smetana Hall)

Beautifully restored venue for symphony concerts in the Obecní dům (Municipal House).

✉ Náměstí Republiky 5, Nové Město ☎ 222 002 336; www.obecnidum.cz
Ⓜ Náměstí Republiky 🚋 5, 14

Státní Opera Praha (State Opera House)

This company performs major Italian, German and Czech operas in a fine, four-tiered auditorium. Performances usually begin at 7pm.

✉ Wilsonova 4, Nové Město ☎ 224 227 266; www.opera.cz Ⓜ Muzeum

Excursions

There are any number of possible excursions from Prague, many within an hour or two's journey by train or car. The variety of scenery may come as a surprise, from the craggy uplands of Český ráj and the Krkonoše (Giant) Mountains to the woodland slopes of the Berounka Valley. Further south around Třeboň is a wetland area of lakes and carp-rearing ponds, an ideal habitat for water birds; and there are other surprises in store: a fairy-tale castle on an isolated hill top, a gloomy limestone cave with dripping stalactites, a charming Renaissance town hall at the centre of a busy market square. The elegant 19th-century resort of Karlovy Vary is famous for its hot mineral springs; Plzeň and České Budějovice are both centres of the brewing industry, and the vineyards of Mělník date back to the reign of Charles IV.

BRNO

The capital of Moravia and the second city of the Republic, Brno is famous for its Motorcycle Grand Prix and trade fairs, but it is also a lively cultural centre with a major university and several theatres (including the Reduta, where Mozart conducted his own compositions in 1767) and some interesting historical sights. Two Brno landmarks – the Špilberk fortress, which for centuries served as a Habsburg prison and is now the city museum, and the Gothic Cathedral of St Peter and St Paul – stand on adjacent hills. Below the cathedral is the Old Town. It's worth climbing the tower of the Old City Hall for the views. Notice the middle turret of the hall's Gothic portal, which is askew: according to the local legend, it was left deliberately crooked by the builder as an act of revenge on the burghers for not paying his wages in full.

www.brno.cz

✉ Informační služba, Radnícká 8 ☎ 542 173 590 🕐 Town Hall: Apr–Sep daily 9–5. Castle: Tue–Sun 9–5 ✋ Inexpensive 🍴 Cafés (£), restaurants (££) 🚆 Praha Hlavní nádraží ❓ Aug–Sep: International Motorcycling Championship

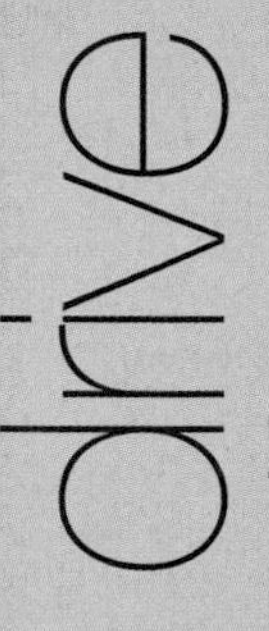

around the Bohemian Uplands

Leave Prague, heading northwards on highway 608 to Bohdanovice, then take highway 9 through Libeznice.

Crossing the River Labe, there are views of the vineyards which cluster around the delightful hillltop town of Mělník (➤ 178).

Continue on highway 9 to Dubá.

On your way you will pass through Liběchov, which has a château dating from 1730.

Turn left onto the 260 to Úštěk.

The ruins of Hrádek Castle will appear on your left as you approach Úštěk. This charming town posseses an attractive elongated square of Gothic and Renaissance houses, as well as the 'birds' cottages' built like nests on rocky promontories by Italian labourers who constructed the railway in the mid-19th century.

Leave Úštěk on highway 260, travelling northwards. This scenic route crosses the forested Central Bohemian Heights (České středohoří), a designated area of natural beauty. At Malé Březno turn left onto highway 261.

The road now tracks between the River Labe and its sandstone cliffs to the industrial town of Ústí nad Labem. On a promontory south of Ústí you will pass Střekov Castle, with its round Gothic tower. It is said to have been the inspiration for Richard Wagner's opera *Tannhäuser.*

Continue on the 261.

Drive through the orchards and hop gardens of the Labe Valley to Litoměřice, an attractive medieval market town with two town halls (Gothic and Renaissance) as well as numerous baroque churches and town houses.

Cross the river and join highway E55 through Terezín *(➤ 182)* *to return to Prague.*

Distance 131km (81 miles)
Time 8 hours
Start/end point Střížkov, Praha 9
Lunch U Tomáše (£) ✉ Náměstí Míru 30, Mělnik ☎ 206 627 357

ČESKÉ BUDĚJOVICE

This sedate old town was founded in 1265 by King Otokar II Přemysl as a base from which to attack his enemies, the unruly Vítkovec clan. During the Hussite Wars the mainly German population remained royalist and stoutly defended the Catholic cause. Commercially, the 16th century was a golden age as České Budějovice exploited its precious silver deposits, but the economic and social dislocation caused by the Thirty Years' War put an end to this prosperity and in 1641 the town was ravaged by a terrible fire which damaged or destroyed almost every building of importance. This led to large-scale reconstruction, which accounts for the mainly baroque appearance of today's town. The advent of the railways in the 19th century brought industry to the region and České Budějovice became the third largest city in the country after Prague and Plzeň. Today it is best known for its beer.

The town's main square, náměstí Přemysla Otakara II, is one of the largest in Europe: the Town Hall, a graceful building dating from 1727 to 1730, the 13th-century Church of St Nicholas and the lofty Černá Věž (Black Tower) are the main attractions. It's a climb of 360 steps to the Tower's viewing gallery, but well worth it. A few minutes' walk away is the old meat market (Masné krámy), dating from 1564, now serving as a traditional beer hall. Visitors who develop a taste for Budvar may like to sign up for a tour of the famous brewery.

www.c-budejovice.cz

Informační centrum: náměstí Přemysla Otakara II 2 386 801 413. Brewery: 387 705 111 Brewery: daily 9–3, for group tours Cafés (£), restaurants (££) Praha Hlavní Nádraží Aug: International Agricultural Show

ČESKÝ KRUMLOV

Český Krumlov is simply ravishing. Surrounded by rolling countryside and the wooded Šumava Hills, the old town – a UNESCO World Heritage Site – nestles in a bend of the Vltava

River. For more than 600 years its fortunes were inseparable from those of the aristocratic families residing in the castle: the lords of Krumlov, the Rožmberks, the Eggenbergs and finally the Schwarzenbergs, who were not dispossessed until after World War II. The castle is part medieval fortress, part château, magnificently set on a clifftop overlooking the town, and boasting a unique bridge resembling an aqueduct, a picture gallery and the oldest private theatre in Europe. Guided tours include a visit to the Hall of Masks, a ballroom painted in 1748 with *trompe-l'oeil* figures of guests attending a masquerade. The houses of the Latrán, the area around the castle, were originally occupied by servants and court scribes. Buildings here include a 14th-century Minorite Monastery and the Eggenberg Brewery, which still makes its deliveries by horse and cart. Below the castle steps is the medieval former hospice and Church of St Jošt, now converted into private apartments.

The nucleus of the town is on the opposite bank of the Vltava. Prominent on náměstí Svornosti (the main square) is the Town Hall, with attractive arcades and vaulting. Vilém of Rožmberk is buried in the Gothic Church of St Vitus, which dates from 1439. The Latin School, now a music school and the former Jesuit College, now the Hotel Růže, are also worth a look.

www.ckrumlov.cz

✉ Tourist Service Rooseveltova 28 ☎ 380 712 853 ⌚ Castle: Apr–May, Sep–Oct Tue–Sun 9–12, 1–4; Jul–Aug Tue–Sun 9–12, 1–5. Tower: Apr–Oct Tue–Sun 9–6 Moderate Cafés (£), restaurants (££) Praha Hlavní nádraží (via České Budějovice) ? Mid-Jun: Five-Petal Rose Festival; Aug: International Music Festival

ČESKÝ ŠTERNBERK

Founded in 1242 on a sheer cliff above the Sázava River, the fortress home of the Šternberk family commands wonderful views of the valley. The castle was remodelled in the baroque style by Italian craftsmen between 1660 and 1670. The rococo Chapel of St Sebastian and the Yellow Room, with an elaborate stucco moulding by Carlo Bentano, are particularly beautiful. There is also a display of silver miniatures and a set of engravings on the staircase which depict scenes from the Thirty Years' War.

Český Šternberk 317 855 101 Jul–Sep Tue–Sun 9–6; May Sat–Sun 9–4; Jun, Oct Tue–Sun 9–5; Nov–Mar Sat–Thu 9–4 Moderate Restaurant (££) Bus from Roztyly metro

HRADEC KRÁLOVÉ

Hradec Králové has been the regional capital of Eastern Bohemia since the 10th century. A Hussite stronghold in the 15th century, the town later featured in the Austro-Prussian war of 1866 as the site of the Battle of Königgrätz. At the heart of the old town is an attractive square (actually triangular in shape) known as Žižkovo náměstí after the Hussite warrior, Jan Žižka, who is buried here. Overlooking the square is the 14th-century Cathedral of the Holy Spirit. The free-standing belfry (71.5m/235ft high) is known as the White Tower, and was added later. Just in front of the tower is a

handsome Renaissance town hall. The Jesuit Church of the Assumption, on the southern side of the square, has an attractive 17th-century interior. Two leading art nouveau architects, Osvald Polívka and Jan Kot, worked in Hradec Králové. Polívka designed the Gallery of Modern Art, while Kot was responsible for the Regional Museum of East Bohemia just outside the Old Town.

www.hradeckralove.org

Hradec Králové Information: 495 534 482 Museum and Gallery: Tue–Sun 9–12, 1–5 Cafés (£), restaurants (££) Praha Hlavní nádraží Information centre: Gočárova třída 1225

KARLOVY VARY

According to legend, Charles IV was out hunting one day when one of his hounds tumbled into a hot spring and the secret of Karlovy Vary was out. In 1522 Dr Payer of Loket set out the properties of the waters in a medical treatise and their fame began to spread. By the end of the 16th century there were more than 200 spa buildings, but the town's present appearance dates mainly from the 19th century.

There are 12 hot mineral springs in all, housed in five colonnades. The best known (and the hottest) is the Vřídlo, at 72°C (161°F), which spurts to a height of 10m (33ft). The wrought-iron Sadová and the neo-Renaissance Mlýnská colonnades preserve something of their 19th-century atmosphere.

Besides the curative waters, Karlovy Vary is famous for another, more potent liquid: a herb liquer called *Becherovka* after the doctor who invented the recipe while working at the spa in the early 1700s. The area comes alive in summer, when there are concerts and festivals.

www.karlovyvary.cz

Lázenská 1 353 224 097 Cafés (£), restaurants (££–£££) Coach from Praha Florenc May: opening of Spa Season; Jul: International Film Festival

KARLŠTEJN

Perched on a cliff above the Berounka River, Karlštejn was founded by Charles IV in 1348 as a treasury for the imperial regalia and his collection of relics. In the 19th century the fortress was remodelled in neo-Gothic style by Joseph Mocker. Rooms open to the public include the wood-panelled Audience Hall, the Luxembourg Hall and the Church of Our Lady, which has a fine timber ceiling and fragments of 14th-century fresco painting. The magnificent Chapel of the Holy Cross in the Great Tower contains copies of 14th-century panels by Master Theodoric (the originals are in St George's Convent in Prague (➤ 113). The walls of the chapel are inlaid with over 2,000 semiprecious stones.

www.hradkarlstejn.cz

Karlštejn 311 681 617 May, Jun, Sep daily 9–12, 12.30–5; Jul–Aug daily 9–12, 12.30–6; Apr, Oct daily 9–12, 1–4; Mar, Tue–Sun 9–12, 1–3; Nov–Dec 9–12, 1–3 Expensive Cafés (£), restaurants (££) near by Karlštejn from Praha-Smíchov Guided tour only

KONOPIŠTĚ

In 1887 Konopiště Castle was acquired by the heir to the Habsburg throne, Franz Ferdinand, for his Czech wife Sophie Chotek. The Archduke's abiding passion was hunting – in a career spanning 40 years he bagged more than 300,000 animals. Some of the trophies line the walls of the Great Hall. Also worth seeing is Franz Ferdinand's impressive collection of medieval arms and armour and the landscaped garden with peacocks grazing on the lawn.

www.konopiste.com

Konopiště 317 721 366 May–Aug Tue–Sun 9–12, 1–5. Check for rest of year Expensive Restaurant (£) Benešov from Praha-Smíchov, then bus Guided tour only

KŘIVOKLÁT

This beautiful 13th-century castle, with its unusual 35m-high (115ft) round tower, was once the royal hunting lodge of Charles IV. Inside is the vaulted King's Hall, a Gothic chapel with a fine carved altarpiece, a dungeon once used as a prison and now home to a grim assortment of torture instruments, and the Knights' Hall, with a collection of late Gothic paintings and sculptures.

www.krivoklat.cz

Křivoklát 313 558 440 Jul–Aug daily 9–12, 1–5; Jun Tue–Sun 9–12, 1–5; May, Sep Tue–Sun 9–12, 1–4; Apr, Oct Tue–Sun 9–12, 1–3; Mar, Nov–Dec Sat–Sun 9–12, 1–3 Moderate Křivoklát from Praha-Smíchov, change at Beroun Guided tour only

KUTNÁ HORA

The name means 'mining mountain', and it was the discovery of large deposits of silver and copper ore in the 13th century which turned Kutná Hora overnight into one of the boom towns of Central Europe. A royal mint, founded at the beginning of the 14th century and known as the Italian Court, after Wenceslas II's Florentine advisors, produced its distinctive silver coin, *Pražské grosé*, until 1547. Visitors to the Court can see art nouveau frescoes in the Wenceslas Chapel, as well as treasures from the Gothic Town Hall, which burned down in 1770, including a brightly painted wooden statue of Christ, *Ecce Homo* (1502). The Cathedral of St Barbara was endowed by the miners and dedicated to their patron saint. Peter Parler's unusual design of three tent-roofed spires supported by a forest of flying buttresses was begun in 1388 but not completed until the end of the 15th century, when Matthias Rejsek and Benedikt Reid built the magnificent vaulted ceiling. Behind the Hrádek museum there is a medieval mine where visitors are shown the *trejv*, a horse-drawn winch used for lifting the bags of ore.

North of Kutná Hora is Sedlec, where, in the 19th century, the Cistercian ossuary was turned into a macabre work of art by František Rint. There are bone monstrances, chandeliers and even a Schwarzenberg coat of arms.

www.kutnahora.cz

Information: Palackého náměstí 377 327 512 378 Italian Court: Nov–Feb daily 10–3.30; Mar, Oct daily 10–4.30; Apr, Sep daily 9–5.30. St Barbara's Cathedral: Nov–Mar Tue–Sun 9–12, 2–3.30; Apr, Oct Tue–Sun

9–12,1–4; May–Sep Tue–Sun 9–5.30. Museum hrádek: Apr, Oct Tue–Sun 9–5; May–Sep Tue–Sun 9–6. Ossuary: Nov–Mar daily 9–12, 1–4; Apr–Sep daily 8–12, 1–6 Cafés (£), restaurants (££–£££) Praha Masarykovo to Sedlec, then bus Coach from Praha Želivského metro station Jun: international guitar competition

LIDICE

In June 1942, following the assassination of the Nazi Governor of Bohemia and Moravia, Reinhard Heydrich, this small village was one of several arbitrarily singled out for reprisal. The men were herded into a farmhouse and shot, the women and children were transported to concentration camps and the entire village was razed to the ground. The site is now a shrine with a museum – a wooden cross and a memorial mark the actual place where the men were shot and buried.

www.lidice-memorial.cz

Památnik Lidice, 273 54 Lidice 312 253 702 Apr–Sep daily 9–6, Oct–Mar daily 9–4 Inexpensive Bus (Kladno line) from Dejvická metro station 10 Jun: memorial day

LITOMYŠL

This attractive town has one of the largest squares in the Czech Republic, with a Gothic Town Hall and Renaissance and baroque houses. 'At the Knights', built in 1540, has a superb sculpted façade: attend an art exhibition here and take a look at the panelled Renaissance ceiling. The château was built between 1568 and 1581. Its exterior is decorated with stunning sgraffiti by Šimon Vlach and the private theatre is one of the oldest in Europe. Litomyšl is also famous as the birthplace of the composer Bedřich Smetana. His apartment in the château is now a museum and music festivals take place in his honour throughout the summer.

Information: Smetanovo náměstí 72 461 612 161 Château: May–Aug Tue–Sun 8–12,1–5; Sep 9–12, 1–4; Apr, Oct Sat–Sun 9–12, 1–4 Inexpensive Jun–Jul: Smetana's Litomyšl (opera festival)

MĚLNÍK

Perched on a hilltop, with commanding views across the confluence of the Vltava and Labe (Elbe) rivers, is the château, Mělník's main tourist attraction. Founded in the 10th century, it originally belonged to the Bohemian royal family and was occupied by several queens, including the wives of John of Luxemburg and Charles IV, who is credited with introducing wine-making to the region. The castle passed into the hands of the Lobkowicz family early in the 17th century and they have owned it intermittently ever since. Mainly of baroque appearance, its northern wing has an impressive Renaissance arcade and loggia with sgraffito decoration, dating from 1555. The rooms have been refurbished in a variety of styles; most interesting is the Large Bedroom, which contains an early 17th-century canopied bed with a painting of the Madonna at the head. Visitors are also shown trophies and mementoes belonging to one of the château's more recent owners, Jiří Christian Lobkowicz, a talented racing driver who died tragically on a track in Berlin in 1932. There is a separate entrance charge for a tour of the 13th-century wine cellars, with tastings.

Mělník's grapes are of the Traminer and Riesling varieties.

You can also tour the Church of St Peter and Paul, built between 1480 and 1520. Its nave is roofed with splendid network and star vaulting and decorated with Renaissance and baroque paintings, including work by Karel Škřeta. The 'pewter' font is actually made of wood. The main draw here is the crypt with its fascinating charnel house, stacked from floor to ceiling with orderly rows of heaped bones – some 15,000 of them at the last count. Some of the skulls are fractured or dented – the result of bullet wounds sustained in the battles of the Thirty Years' War.

www.melnik.cz

✉ Turistické Informační st: náměstí Mirů ☎ 315 627 503; château: 315 622 121 🕐 Château: May, Jun, Sep Tue–Sun 9–5; Jul–Aug Tue–Sun 9–6 Moderate Cafés and restaurants (£–£££) Bus from Florenc coach station, Prague

PLZEŇ

Beer has been brewed in Plzeň since 1295 and the Pilsner Urquell brewery is the main attraction in this largely industrial town. The guided tour of the cellars (there are 9km/5.5 miles in all) includes a visit to the extravagantly decorated beer hall, definitely an experience not to be missed. Close by is a fascinating Museum of Brewing housed, appropriately enough, in a medieval malthouse.

Plzeň's main square, náměstí Republiky, has some fine Renaissance and baroque town houses and is dominated by the Gothic Cathedral of St Bartholomew, which has the tallest steeple in the country (102m/335ft).

www.plzen-city.cz

✉ Information: náměstí Republiky 41 ☎ Brewery: 378 035 330. Museum: 377 235 574. Brewery visitor centre: 377 062 888 🕐 Brewery: daily 12.30 and 2pm unless booked in advance. Pivovarské Muzeum: daily 10–6 Moderate Cafés (£), restaurants (££) Praha Hlavní nádraží

TÁBOR

In a marvellous situation on a bluff commanding the Lužnice Valley, Tábor takes its name from the biblical mountain where Christ is said to have appeared transfigured to his disciples. After the death of Jan Hus, the Hussites transferred their allegiance to the one-eyed general Jan Žižka, who continued the struggle against the Catholics. He encamped here in 1420 and held out successfuly for four years until his death in battle. The town's attractive main square, about 20 minutes' walk from the station, is named after him and there is a statue by Josef Strachovksý.

The tower of the Church of the Transfiguration, which dates from the 16th century, offers the best views of the gabled Renaissance and classical houses and of the town itself, which is seen melting into the distance.

An exhibition in the neo-Gothic Town Hall presents an excellent account of the Hussite Movement. Don't miss the tour of the labyrinthine tunnels, 600m (1,968ft) below ground. Dating from the 15th century, they were used variously as beer cellars, as a prison for unruly women and as an escape route in time of war. When you emerge, you'll find yourself near a café where you can sit and relax. The narrow twisting streets

of the Old Town are a delight, although you may get lost from time to time. This is no accident – when the town was laid out Žižka's followers wanted to make life as confusing as possible for the enemy. A pleasant stroll along the banks of the Lužnice River leads to the Bechyňe Gate and Kotnov Castle, with its distictive round tower. Inside are some fascinating displays on medieval life in the region, with costumes, archaeological finds, farming implements and weapons. The views from the tower are a bonus.

Only 2km (1 mile) away, across beautiful countryside, is the hamlet of Klokoty, with a baroque convent and church dating from the early 18th century. The wayside shrines along the footpath mark it out as a place of Catholic pilgrimage.

On the other side of town, between Žižkovo and Tržní náměstí, is a Renaissance water tower decorated with vaulted gables and dating from 1497.

The water was pumped to the town's seven fountains from the Jordan, the oldest dam in Europe, via a system of wooden pipes.

www.tabor.cz

Infocentrum: Žižkovo náměstí 2 381 486 230 Town Hall Museum: Apr–Oct daily 8.30–5; Nov–Mar Mon–Fri 8.30–5 Inexpensive Cafés (£), restaurants (££) Praha Hlavní nádraží Sep: Tábor Meetings, a festival of parades, music and events

TEREZÍN

In 1942 the Nazis turned Terezín into a ghetto and transit camp for Jews. More than 150,000 people ended up in extermination camps, while a further 35,000 died of disease and starvation. At the same time the Germans used Terezín for their perverted propaganda purposes, persuading Red Cross visitors that this was a flourishing cultural and commercial centre. The exhibition in the main fortress, now restored after the flood, gives an excellent if

harrowing account of the realities of life in the camp, while across the river, in the lesser fortress, visitors can tour the barracks, workshops, isolation cells, mortuaries, execution grounds and former mass graves.

www.pamatnik-terezin.cz

Information: Principova alej 304 416 782 225 Apr–Oct daily 9–6; Nov–Mar daily 9–5.30 Moderate Restaurant (£) Coach from Praha Florenc

TŘEBOŇ

The charming spa town of Třeboň is best known for the quality of its carp ponds, which date back to the 14th century – Carp Rožmberk is on the menu of many restaurants even today. Four surviving gates lead into the walled Old Town, which has at its heart a beautiful, elongated square. Dating from 1566, the Town Hall is decorated with three coats of arms: those of the town and its wealthy patrons, the Rožmberks and the Schwarzenbergs. Opposite is the 16th-century White Horse Inn, which has an unusual turreted gable. Třeboň has its own brewery and horse-drawn drays deliver Regent beer to the local hotels and restaurants. The Augustinian monastery church of St Giles dates from 1367 and contains a number of Gothic features, including a statue of the Madonna. The attractive Renaissance château is open to the public and was built in 1562 by the Rožmberk family.

Information: Masarykovo náměstí 103 384 721 169 Château: May–Sep Tue–Sun 9–noon, 1–5 Cafés (£), restaurants (££) Praha Hlavní nádraží

Index

Acknowledgements

The Automobile Association would like to thank the following photographers and companies for their assistance in the preparation of this book.

Abbreviations for the picture credits are as follows – (t) top; (b) bottom; (c) centre; (l) left; (r) right; (AA) AA World Travel Library

4l River Vltava seen from Letna, AA/Jonathan Smith; **4c** Mala Strana metro station, AA/Jon Wyand; **4r** St Vitus Cathedral, AA/Simon McBride; **5l** Waldstein Palace, AA/Clive Sawyer; **5c** Charles Bridge, AA/Simon McBride; **5r** Cesky Krumlov, AA/Jon Wyand; **6/7** River Vltava seen from Letna, AA/Jonathan Smith; **8/9** Astronomical Clock, Old Town Square, AA/Clive Sawyer; **10/11t** Old Town, AA/Simon McBride; **10bl** Male Namesti, Old Town, AA/Jonathan Smith; **10/11b** Old Town Square, AA/Jonathan Smith; **11c** Tram, AA/Jonathan Smith; **12bl** Traditional food, AA/Jonathan Smith; **12br** Old Town Square, AA/Simon McBride; **13tl** Sandwich bar, AA/Jon Wyand; **13tr** Bakery, AA/Jonathan Smith; **13b** Obecni Dum, Old Town, AA/Jonathan Smith; **14l** Evropa Hotel, Wenceslas Square, AA/Jon Wyand; **14br** Pilsner Urquell lager, AA/Jon Wyand; **15tl** Cafe Imperial, New Town, AA/Jonathan Smith; **15cr** Astronomical Clock, Old Town, AA/Simon McBride; **15bl** Absinthe, AA/Jonathan Smith; **16** Charles Bridge, AA/Simon McBride; **17** Figures on astronomical clock, Old Town Square, AA/Clive Sawyer; **18tl** Beer tap, U Zlatecho Tygra, AA/Simon McBride; **18/19t** Royal Gardens seen from the Belvedere, AA/Simon McBride; **18/19b** Estates Theatre, AA/Clive Sawyer; **20/21** Mala Strana metro station, AA/Jon Wyand; **24** Obecni dum, AA/Jon Wyand; **25** Old Town Square, AA/Simon McBride; **26t** Plane, Digitalvision; **27** Traffic on Jiraskuv most, AA/Jonathan Smith; **28** River Vltava, AA/Jonathan Smith; **29t** Tram, AA/Jonathan Smith; **30** Telephone, AA/Simon McBride; **32** Post box, AA/Jonathan Smith; **34/35** St Vitus and Prague Castle, AA/Simon McBride; **36b** St Nicholas, Mala Strana, AA/Tony Souter; **37t** View from Mala Strana area towards Charles Bridge, AA/Simon McBride; **38c** Franz Kafka memorial, Dusni, AA/Jonathan Smith; **38/39** Josefov, AA/Simon McBride; **39br** Old Jewish Cemetery, AA/Simon McBride; **40cl** St Vitus Cathedral, AA/Simon McBride; **40bl** St Vitus, AA/Tony Souter; **41t** St Vitus Cathedral, AA; **41b** Alfons Mucha window, St Vitus, AA/Jon Wyand; **42** Loreta, AA/Simon McBride; **43** Loreta, AA/Simon McBride; **44t** Prague Castle, AA/Jonathan Smith; **44c** Castle Gardens, AA/Clive Sawyer; **44/45b** Prague Castle, AA/Jonathan Smith; **45tl** Chapel of the Holy Cross, Prague Castle, AA/Clive Sawyer; **46** Astronomical clock, Old Town Square, AA/Clive Sawyer; **47** Astronomical clock, Old Town Square, AA/Simon McBride; **48** German paintings, Sternbersky Palac, AA/Jonathan Smith; **50bc** Strahov Gospel, Strahov Monastery, AA/Simon McBride; **50/51** Philosophical Hall, Strahov Monastery, AA/Simon McBride; **51r** Strahov Monastery, AA/Simon McBride; **52** Wenceslas Square, AA/Simon McBride; **53** Wenceslas Square, AA/Jonathan Smith; **54** Veletrzni Palac, AA/Jonathan Smith; **55/56** Atrium view, Veletrzni Palac, AA/Jonathan Smith; **56/57** Waldstein Palace, AA/Clive Sawyer; **58/59** Ice hockey supporters, Old Town Square, AA/Jonathan Smith; **60** U Kalicha, AA/Tony Souter; **62/63** Marathon runners AA/Jonathan Smith; **64/65** View from Petrin Hill, AA/Clive Sawyer; **66** Tyn Church, Old Town Square, AA/Simon McBride; **67** Nerudova street, AA/Jonathan Smith; **68/69** Cernin Palace, AA/Clive Sawyer; **70/71** St Nicholas Church, Old Town, AA/Simon McBride; **73** Wooden toys, AA/Jonathan Smith; **74** Gardens beneath Prague Castle, AA/Simon McBride; **76** Aria Hotel; **78** Bata shop window, AA/Jonathan Smith; **80/81** Charles Bridge, AA/Simon McBride; **83** Old Town Square, AA/Jonathan Smith; **85** Bethlehem Chapel, AA/Tony Souter; **86t** Black Madonna House, AA/Jonathan Smith; **86c** Black Madonna in her cage, AA/Clive Sawyer; **87b** House at the Stone Bell, AA/Jon Wyand; **88** Charles Bridge, AA/Jon Wyand; **89** Karolinum, AA/Clive Sawyer; **90** Library, Klementinum, AA/Jonathan Smith; **91** Klementinum, AA/Jonathan Smith; **92** Charles IV, Knights of the Cross Square, AA/Simon McBride; **93** St Saviour, Knights of the Cross Square, AA/Simon McBride; **94/95t** River Vltava and Smetana Museum (on left), AA/Simon McBride; **94b** Bedrich Smetana statue, AA/Jon Wyand; **96t** Old Town Square, AA/Simon McBride; **96b** Jan Hus monument, AA/Jon Wyand; **97b** Estates Theatre, AA/Jon Wyand; **98t** Ungelt, AA/Jonathan Smith; **98b** Wine Shop Ungelt, AA/Jonathan Smith; **107** St George's Convent and Basilica, AA/Jonathan Smith; **108** Mozart Museum, AA/Jon Wyand; **109t** Memorial to the Battle of the White Mountain, AA/Jon Wyand; **109b** Brevnov Monastery, AA/Jon Wyand; **110** Cernin Palace, AA/Jon Wyand; **111t** Hradcany Square, AA/Jon Wyand; **111b** Hradcany Square, AA/Clive Sawyer; **112** Crypt, Basilica of St George, AA/Jon Wyand; 113 St George's Convent, AA/Jonathan Smith; **114** Church of Our Lady of Victory, AA/Tony Souter; **115** Spire, Church of St Thomas, AA/Clive Sawyer; **116t** The Royal Gardens, AA/Simon McBride; **116b** Singing Fountain, Royal Gardens, AA/Simon McBride; **117** Lapidarium, AA/Clive Sawyer; **118** John Lennon Wall, AA/Jon Wyand; **119** Malostranske Namesti, AA/Simon McBride; **120** National Technical Museum, AA/Jon Wyand; **121** Nerudova, AA/Jon Wyand; **122** Cerninska street, Novy Svet, AA/Jonathan Smith; **123** Church of St Lawrence, Kinsky Garden, Petrin Hill, AA/Jon Wyand; **124** Certovka, AA/Simon McBride; **125** Lesser Quarter, AA/Simon McBride; **126t** Troja Chateau, AA/Clive Sawyer; **126c** Troja Chateau, AA/Jon Wyand; **127** Waldstein Gardens, AA/Clive Sawyer; **128** Exhibition Hall, Vystaviste, AA/Clive Sawyer; **129** Golden Lane,

AA/Simon McBride; **134** Old-New Synagogue, AA/Simon McBride; **135t** Church of Sv. Salvator, St Agnes's Convent, AA/Jonathan Smith; **135b** Altarpiece "Resurrection" by the Master of the Trebon, St Agnes's Convent, AA/Jonathan Smith; **136l** Expozice F Kafky, AA/Jon Wyand; **136/137** Old Jewish Cemetery, AA/Simon McBride; **139** Maiselova Synagoga, AA/Jonathan Smith; **140** Ceremonial Hall, AA/Tony Souter; **141** Pinkas Synagogue, AA/Jonathan Smith/Jewish Museum, Prague; **142** Rudolfinum, AA/Simon McBride; **143l** Old-New Synagogue, AA/Jon Wyand; **143r** Old-New Synagogue and Jewish Town Hall, AA/Simon McBride; **144** Old Jewish Cemetery, AA/Tony Souter; **147** Church of St Cyril and St Methodius, AA/Jonathan Smith; **148** Church of Our Lady of the Snows, AA/Jon Wyand; **149** Memorial to the parachutists, Church of SS Cyril and Methodius, AA/Clive Sawyer; **150** Old Town Square in winter (1862) painting by Ferdinand Lepie, Muzeum Hlavniho Mesta Prahy, AA/Jonathan Smith; **151** Bust of Stalin, Museum of Communism, AA/Jonathan Smith; **153** National Theatre, AA/Jonathan Smith; **154** National Museum, AA/Jon Wyand; **155** Obecni Dum, AA/Simon McBride; **157** Powder Tower, AA/Clive Sawyer; **158** Church of St Peter and St Paul, AA/Clive Sawyer; **164/165** Cesky Krumlov, AA/Jon Wyand; **167** Brno, AA/Jon Wyand; **168** Church of St Peter and Paul, Melnik, AA/Jon Wyand; **169t** Town Hall, Melnik, AA/Jon Wyand; **171** Cesky Krumlov, AA/Jon Wyand; **172b** Hradec Kralove, AA/J Wyand; **172/173c** Karlovy Vary, AA/Jon Wyand; **174** Karlstejn Castle, AA/Clive Sawyer; **176** Kutna Hora, AA/Jon Wyand; **178** Melnik, AA/Jon Wyand; **179** Plzen, AA/Jon Wyand; **180/181** Equestrian statue of Jan Zizka, Tabor, AA/Jon Wyand; **182** Gravestones, Terezin, AA/Jon Wyand.

Every effort has been made to trace the copyright holders, and we apologise in advance for any accidental errors. We would be happy to apply the corrections in the following edition of this publication.

Street Index

Dear Reader

Your comments, opinions and recommendations are very important to us. So please help us to improve our travel guides by taking a few minutes to complete this simple questionnaire.

You do not need a stamp (unless posted outside the UK). If you do not want to cut this page from your guide, then photocopy it or write your answers on a plain sheet of paper.

Send to: **The Editor, AA World Travel Guides, FREEPOST SCE 4598, Basingstoke RG21 4GY.**

Your recommendations...

We always encourage readers' recommendations for restaurants, nightlife or shopping – if your recommendation is used in the next edition of the guide, we will send you a **FREE AA Guide** of your choice from this series. Please state below the establishment name, location and your reasons for recommending it.

____

____

____

____

____

____

Please send me **AA Guide** ______________________________

About this guide...

Which title did you buy?

AA ______________________________

Where did you buy it? ______________________________

When? mm / y y

Why did you choose this guide? ______________________________

____

____

____

____

Did this guide meet your expectations?

Exceeded ☐ Met all ☐ Met most ☐ Fell below ☐

Were there any aspects of this guide that you particularly liked? ______________________________

____

____

____

continued on next page...

Is there anything we could have done better? ______________________________

____

____

____

About you...

Name (*Mr/Mrs/Ms*) ______________________________

Address ______________________________

____

______________________________ Postcode

Daytime tel nos ______________________________

Email ______________________________

Please only give us your mobile phone number or email if you wish to hear from us about other products and services from the AA and partners by text or mms, or email.

Which age group are you in?

Under 25 ☐ 25–34 ☐ 35–44 ☐ 45–54 ☐ 55–64 ☐ 65+ ☐

How many trips do you make a year?

Less than one ☐ One ☐ Two ☐ Three or more ☐

Are you an AA member? Yes ☐ No ☐

About your trip...

When did you book? mm / y y When did you travel? mm / y y

How long did you stay? ______________________________

Was it for business or leisure? ______________________________

Did you buy any other travel guides for your trip?

If yes, which ones? ______________________________

____

____

Thank you for taking the time to complete this questionnaire. Please send it to us as soon as possible, and remember, you do not need a stamp (*unless posted outside the UK*).

The information we hold about you will be used to provide the products and services requested and for identification, account administration, analysis, and fraud/loss prevention purposes. More details about how that information is used is in our privacy statement, which you'll find under the heading "Personal Information" in our terms and conditions and on our website: www.theAA.com. Copies are also available from us by post, by contacting the Data Protection Manager at AA, Fanum House, Basing View, Basingstoke, Hampshire RG21 4EA.

We may want to contact you about other products and services provided by us, or our partners (by mail, telephone or email) but please tick the box if you DO NOT wish to hear about such products and services from us by mail, telephone or email. ☐